Contents

Sounds of Music

Acknowledgements

Music

Coffee
Words and Music by Kenneth Simpson © Novello & Company Limited.

Divali Song
Words and Music by George Odam © Silver Burdett Ginn.

The Inch Worm
Words and Music by Frank Loesser © 1951, 1952 Frank Music Corporation. © renewed 1979, 1980 Frank Music Corporation. Published and administered by MPL Communications Limited. Used by permission of Music Sales Limited. All Rights Reserved. International Copyright Secured.

Mistletoe and Wine
Music by Keith Strachan. Words by Leslie Stewart & Jeremy Paul © 1988 Patch Music Limited. All rights administered by Peermusic (UK) Limited, 8-14 Verulam Street, London WC1. Used by permission of Music Sales Limited. All Rights Reserved. International Copyright Secured.

Notin' Around
Words and Music by George Odam © Georgian Music DTP.

Polish the Old Menorah
Words and Music by Joan Arnold © Georgian Music DTP.

Sing a March
Words and Music by Ed J Hermann © Prentice Hall.

Summer Holiday
Words and Music by Bruce Welch / Brian Bennett © 1963, Reproduced by permission of EMI Music Publishing Ltd trading as Elstree Music.

Thank You For The Music
Words and Music by Andersson / Elvaeus © BOCU Music.

This is Our Country
Words and Music by George Odam © Silver Burdett Ginn.

We're Going to the Country
Words and Music by Lionel Bart © 1962 EMI United Partnership Limited, London WC2H 0EA. Worldwide print rights controlled by Warner Bros Publications Inc/IMP Limited.

Wenn Eine Tannigi Hose Het
Words and Music by Otto Mller-Blum © Musikverlag Zum Pelikan, Hug & Co., Musikverlage, Zrich.

The White Cliffs of Dover
Words by Nat Burton. Music by Walter Kent © 1941, Shapiro Bernstein & Co. Inc., USA. Reproduced by permission of B Feldman & Co Ltd., London WC2H 0EA.

And the World Keeps Turning Around
Words and Music by Susan Stevens © 1980, Reproduced by permission of EMI Music Publishing Ltd., London WC2H 0EA.

Artwork

Using classroom musical instruments: Artwork by Angela Lumley

Photocopy sheets
Photocopy sheet artwork by Angela Lumley

Posters
Poster 1: Bluebell Railway, Sheffield Park © Alain le Garsmeur/Collections; Fan vaulting, ceiling of Divinity School, Oxford © Anne Gordon/Collections; Wickerwork © Overalls/Collections; *Clematis Chrysocoma* © Eric Crichton/Bruce Coleman Ltd.
Poster 2: Fireworks © Brian Shuel/Collections; Trafalgar Square Christmas tree © Brian Shuel/ Collections; Hanukah © L. Taylor/The Hutchison Library; Divali lights © L. Taylor/The Hutchison Library.
Poster 3: Blues musicians © Glenn A. Baker Archive/ Redferns Music Library; Shaker room reproduced by permission of the American Museum in Britain, Bath ©; *Carousel* poster © BFI Still, Posters and Designs/20th Century Fox.
Poster 4: artwork by John York.
Poster 5: *Swinging* by Kandinsky © The Tate Gallery, ADAGP, Paris and DACS, London 1996.
Poster 6: Brass band © Phil Chisholm, photographer for the *British Bandsman*.

Every effort has been made to trace all the copyright holders but if any have been inadvertently overlooked the publishers will be pleased to make the necessary arrangement at the first opportunity.

Sounds of Music

TEACHER'S BOOK

First published in 1996 by:

Stanley Thornes Publishers Ltd
Ellenborough House
Wellington Street
CHELTENHAM
GL50 1YW

00 01 02 03 04 / 10 9 8 7 6 5 4 3

A catalogue record for this book is available from the British Library.

ISBN 0 7487 2298 X

Designed and typeset by Oxford Designers & Illustrators
Printed in Great Britain by Antony Rowe Ltd., Chippenham, Wiltshire

General introduction

This programme of music education materials provides strong support for general class teachers in any primary school, especially those who believe they have little or no specialist skills in the subject. Building on our experience in writing music education publications we have focused particularly on practical music-making for all, through singing and associated listening and composing projects, and include newly commissioned songs alongside traditional ones. Listening materials are selected from a wide range of music covering many cultures alongside the western 'classical' tradition and these are enhanced by specially designed visual display materials, promoting discussion and appraising. Full-colour posters and numerous photocopiable sheets provide teachers with practical aids to music learning, complementing high-quality sound recordings.

Sounds of Music assumes that the school has only a minimum of equipment, but that this will include access to some pitched and non-pitched percussion. Recorder work will be acknowledged and encouraged, although it will not be integral to the success of any lesson, and the materials, through differentiation, will encourage children with special instrumental skills to use them in the classroom. Singing is at the heart of the programme and this repertoire is attractive and progressive, encouraging unison singing at Key Stage 1/P1–3 and continuing to some singing in parts during Key Stage 2/P4–7. With the help of specially made recordings, teachers will be able to support the singing of rounds and songs with more than one part.

Music is an essential programme of study in our schools and these materials provide a basis of classroom work throughout Key Stages 1 and 2/P1–3 and P4–7. In addition, *Sounds of Music* encourages an enhancement of the public identity of the school through corporate listening, performing in assemblies and acts of worship, and in mounting displays and performances for parents and the wider community.

Although the sequence of materials assumes that the ultimate choice and balance of programming is the teacher's responsibility, and that all teachers will include in their plans material of their own particular to the needs of the children, community and region, *Sounds of Music* provides a sequenced and progressive set of lessons accessible to all teachers. The lessons are placed in units of roughly half a term each and the notional teacher-directed lesson is normally assumed to be of no more than one hour in length. Suggestions for individual and group work extend this. It is assumed that challenges will be set up for the class during the teacher-directed lesson and that a strategy will be employed by the teacher to allow individuals, pairs and groups to work on their own during the week.

Sounds of Music is written to be compatible with the most recent National Curriculum documents of England, Wales, Scotland and Northern Ireland. It aims to be user-friendly in every way and to provide teachers not only with a basis for their classroom programme but also for its assessment.

How to use Sounds of Music

Sounds of Music is divided into seven levels, covering Nursery & Reception to Year 6 in England and Wales, and P1 to P7 in Scotland. This level has been written for use in Year 6/P7 classes.

COMPONENTS

Sounds of Music Year 6/P7 level comprises one teacher's book, three compact discs and six posters.

Teacher's Book

This book contains all the support you need to deliver a complete, balanced music curriculum, in line with national educational requirements. Correlations with the National Curriculum (England and Wales) and Expressive Arts 5–14 (Scotland) are on pages 162–166, and advice on planning, progression and assessment is on page 8.

Each lesson is written assuming that the teacher has very little musical training and experience, but naturally you will bring your own skills and experience to the lesson. You will probably want to adapt some of the suggestions to make them especially appropriate for your class.
The consistent layout of the lesson plan pages makes *Sounds of Music* easy to use.

lesson content and objectives clearly stated

resources listed to help with preparation

basic lesson plan designed with non-specialists in mind

ideas for follow up through the week

differentiation by task — differentiation by outcome also built in

suggestions for assessment

additional watertight support and information

MUSICAL ELEMENTS
Pitch; Duration; Tempo

UNIT 1
MOVING PARTS
LESSON 2

SPECIFIC OBJECTIVES
■ Improvising a metre-in-three rhythm pattern ■ Improvising a waltz tune ■ Recognising intervals

Composing A Slow Waltz

KEY WORDS
Leap, interval

RESOURCES
■ CD 1 Track 1 'Inch Worm' ■ Non-pitched instruments ■ Pitched instruments with B♭/A# ■ Tape recorder

ACTIVITIES

WATCHPOINTS

■ *Finding intervals*
Ask the class to sit in a circle with a collection of instruments (pitched and non-pitched) in the middle. Play Track 1 and remind the class of how the melody leaps on the words 'Inch worm, Inch worm, measuring the marigolds'. Explain that the musical term for a 'leap' or 'step' is an 'interval'. Challenge individuals to find the 'Inch worm' intervals on pitched percussion, and to play them at the right time with the recording. **W1**

W1 *The pitches for these intervals are indicated on Photocopy sheet 2.*

■ *Improvising*
Ask a small group of children to make up a slow metre-in-three rhythm pattern with non-pitched instruments. When this is secure, invite a volunteer to improvise a melody on top. Challenge them to include some leaps in the melody and to repeat short patterns or phrases. Give as many turns as time allows. **W2**

W2 *You will probably find that it is the most confident children who volunteer and that they will need much encouragement and several attempts before they achieve a tune that they can remember and repeat. Be satisfied with modest attempts at first.*

FOLLOW UP
Divide the class into groups of about six and give them time to practise, first setting up a slow metre-in-three rhythm pattern and then an individual improvising a melody. Record each attempt and then spend time evaluating their work. Did they keep a steady beat — metre-in-three? Did they play slowly? Did anyone manage to improvise a melody?

EXTENSION ACTIVITIES
Challenge those who learn instruments to use them for improvising their melodies and to find and include some 'Inch worm' intervals.

SUPPORT ACTIVITIES
Do not insist on the shy children improvising in front of the whole class. Work with them individually in a quiet space, playing a slow waltz beat for them while they experiment to find a melody.

ASSESSMENT POINTS
Make a note of those children who:
• recognise and can find the 'Inch worm' intervals; • can improvise a waltz rhythm; • can improvise a waltz tune.

13

In addition to the lesson plans, the Teacher's Book contains Photocopy Sheets which may be photocopied for use in the classroom. The use of these sheets is very varied. Sometimes all the children will need copies, while at other times only those following the Extension Activities will require them. In some cases the sheets should be enlarged if possible, coloured, cut up and made into flash cards.

Also in the Teacher's Book are piano accompaniments, advice on using percussion instruments, a glossary and a classified index.

Compact Discs

All the music referred to in the Teacher's Book — both songs and listening selections — is provided on three CDs, in the order in which it appears in the book. The advantages offered by compact discs are obvious: apart from their durability, the remote control makes them easy for you to use in the classroom, and the search facility enables you to find the right track every time. Most importantly, the quality of sound is the best available which is, of course, what your children deserve.

The songs have been recorded by groups of children and are intended to provide a good model for your children's singing, and you will find it relatively easy to teach the songs to your pupils with the support of the recordings. We have used 'received pronunciation' but your children should try to sing clearly and accurately in whatever accent comes naturally to them. The songs have been recorded at the speed you will want to aim for with your children, but sometimes you may want to practise more slowly without the CD. Many of the lessons suggest joining in with little bits of a song first, before going on to sing the whole thing when the children are ready.

The song accompaniments are in a wide variety of styles, so that each song is stimulating and satisfying musically. When they know a song well, your children can sing along with the accompaniment without the support of the singing on the CD. If you have a balance control on your CD player you can remove the singing by turning the control to the right, because all the singing comes from the left speaker and all the accompaniments come from the right. Where a song has more than one vocal part it has been recorded twice; once in the usual way, and once with the parts on separate tracks. Your children can experience part-singing as they sing one part and the recording plays the other(s).

The listening selections in *Sounds of Music* cover a wide range of music from different times and places. The commercial recordings of western classical music are the best available, and we have searched out recordings of music of many cultures. Different styles of contemporary music are included, as are environmental sounds.

Please note that it is illegal to make copies of the CDs under any circumstances. Additional CDs are available.

Posters

There are six full-colour, A2-size posters for the Year 6/P7 level. They provide stimulus for discussion work, and help the children to understand musical and other concepts. Each poster has a specific musical purpose, explained in the relevant lesson, but you are sure to see many more general uses for them in your classroom.

We hope you and your children will enjoy using *Sounds of Music*.

Planning, progression and assessment

From the very start of a child's music education in the nursery, there is a link between the musical growth of the child and its physical and mental development. Music education also contributes to the child's spiritual, moral, social and cultural development.

Although there is no statutory assessment in the early years of learning, planning and assessment are still integral to the teaching process. To make decisions about what and how to teach, you have to make judgements about what and how children learn, their levels of progress and achievement and their consequent learning needs.

In *Sounds of Music*, there are various suggestions to help you with this teaching process. At the start of each unit, 'About the Unit' indicates the opportunities for learning and includes references both to the main musical elements and to the principal musical activities of performing, composing, listening and appraising. From this you can sketch out the broad aims for the series of lessons or the topic to be taught. Further suggestions are made in the form of three or four general questions which outline the particular emphasis for the next unit, and indicate assessment points to look out for.

In selecting the focus of your lessons, it is not necessary to use the units in the sequence in which they are written. You may choose the one which most closely matches your curriculum programme or topic or the one which builds on the children's experience and develops their skills in order for them to make progress. Equally, you may wish to use additional songs from other units, if they reinforce the concept you are teaching, match your topic or are just good songs to sing.

However, the lessons themselves provide the main clue to the more detailed, individual planning for progression that you will wish to undertake to meet the needs of the individual children in the class.

In each lesson several assessment points are identified. These relate closely to the specific objectives set out at the start of the lesson plan and provide broad coverage of the musical elements. Concentrate on these or some of these objectives to assess what the children can do. It is not intended that you will necessarily make

assessments on all the children at any one time. Nor is it practical to concentrate on more than a few points. However, there will be occasions in each lesson when particular children will achieve, demonstrate understanding or show skills, which will be worth remembering and noting down. You will, over a period of time, build up knowledge about the children which will help your future planning, so that the tasks you set take account of the children's abilities and levels of skill development.

The assessment points are there to guide and to prompt rather than as requirements. You may find it helpful to keep a class music notebook in which to record what individual children achieve. A simple system would be to have a page for each child. Not only does this help you remember the detail of what a child achieves (so, for example, note can be made of accurate singing or sensitive interpretation), but also it ensures that over a period of time each child will receive at least one comment. An empty page means that you need to check that child.

At the end of each lesson are some suggestions for the kind of assessment information that might be applicable. Of course, you may well identify other skills and achievements which are demonstrated in the lesson and these are just as valuable to record. From this list it will also be useful to make a note of skills or activities which need special reinforcement for specific children. These 'targets' can be identified and planned for individuals, small groups or even whole classes, alongside the next set of lesson objectives, thus promoting progression.

In the final years of primary schooling, children's knowledge and understanding can be extended by more focused work on listening and appraising and by injecting greater challenge into performing and composing activities. You will find that some lessons and some activities are planned to do this, by touching on early secondary material. Nevertheless, there should still be an emphasis on enjoyment—of singing and playing together, of experimenting and of sharing feelings and emotions—so important in this aesthetic subject.

About Unit 1
Moving parts

All the songs in this unit allow the children to develop their ability to sing in parts. They are structured in different ways, some with descants, some with parts which are in layers and some with parts which weave in and out of each other. The listening extracts introduce the children to the baroque concerto form and give them the opportunity to learn a little about the musical life of Europe in the seventeenth century.

This unit focuses on concepts which are further developed in Unit 4: texture, timbre and structure.

Lessons
1 Inch Worm
2 Composing A Slow Waltz
3 Notin' Around
4 Concertos
5 Weaving Melodies
6 Silver Moon
7 Turn Turn

TARGETS FOR UNIT 1

The following questions will help you identify what the children know, understand and can do, with an emphasis on their growing awareness of the musical elements in their listening, and their ability to use appropriate musical language when they share their opinions about music.

- How well do the children use musical language to describe the music they hear?
- How do they demonstrate their understanding of the historical and cultural background to the music they hear?
- How well do they apply ideas about structure in their composing?
- How proficient are they in singing in parts?

The Inch Worm

Words and music by Frank Loesser

Slowly

p

Two and two are four, four and four are eight,

5

That's all you have on your bus' - ness - like mind.

9

Two and two are four, four and four are eight,

13

How can you be so blind?_____

17 **Descant**

pp

Two and two are four, four and four are eight,

21

Eight and eight are six - teen, six - teen and six - teen are thir - ty - two.

Two and two are four, four and four are eight,
C A B♭ G

Inch-worm, Inch-worm, mea - sur - ing the mar - i-golds,

Eight and eight are six - teen, six - teen and six - teen are thir - ty- two.

You and your a - rith - me- tic, you'll prob-a - bly go far.

Two and two are four, four and four are eight,

Inch-worm, Inch-worm, mea - sur - ing the mar - i-golds,

Eight and eight are six - teen, six - teen and six - teen are thir - ty- two.

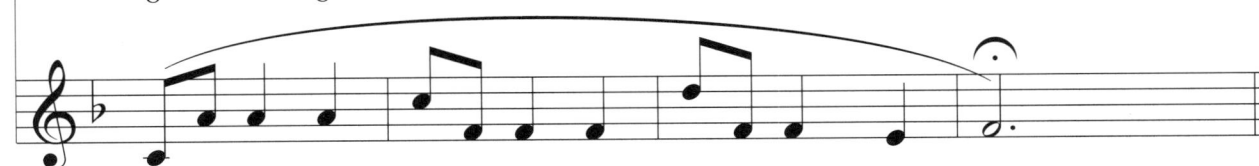

Seems to me you'd stop and see how beau-ti - ful they are.

UNIT 1
MOVING PARTS
LESSON 1

Inch Worm

MUSICAL ELEMENTS
Pitch; Duration; Dynamics; Tempo; Timbre; Texture

SPECIFIC OBJECTIVES
■ Recognising and responding to metre-in-three ■ Discussing mood, tempo and dynamics ■ Singing expressively ■ Singing a descant

KEY WORDS
Descant, solo, waltz, tenor, phrase

RESOURCES
■ CD 1 Tracks 1 and 2 'Inch Worm' ■ Pitched instrument with B♭/A#
■ Photocopy Sheets 1 and 2 ■ Space for movement

ACTIVITIES	WATCHPOINTS

■ *Appraising and responding to the music*

Play Track 2 and ask the children to decide whether it is fast or slow *(slow)*, loud or quiet *(quiet)*, and metre-in-two or three *(3)*.

Let them listen several times and ask them to tell you anything else that they notice about the music and how it makes them feel (mood). *(There may be a number of different observations such as dreamy, sleepy mood; gentle singing by a man's voice (tenor); melody moves in leaps with some repeats; descant is sung above the main tune.)*

Once you have established that the song is in metre-in-three, ask the children to move to the slow beat doing a waltz step. **W1**

W1 *Waltz step: Left, right, together; right, left, together; etc.*

■ *Singing the melody*

Give out Photocopy sheets 1 and 2, and when the children have heard Track 2 through several times, encourage them to sing the melody with the solo tenor. **W2**

Help them to pitch the big leaps in by playing the two patterns on a pitched instrument, low to high:

W2 *Turn the balance control to the right to focus on the melody (man); turn it to the left to focus on the descant (children).*

C   A   B♭   G   C   A   B♭   G
Inch- worm, Inch- worm, mea-suring the mar-i-golds

Encourage them to use one breath for each phrase and to sing quietly and smoothly.

FOLLOW UP
Practise singing the melody with Track 1, turning the balance control to the right to remove the recorded singers. Add the descant part (see Extension).

EXTENSION ACTIVITIES
Use Track 2 to help a small group of more confident singers to learn the descant. Ask them to sing it while the rest of the class sings the melody.

SUPPORT ACTIVITIES
Help less well co-ordinated children to practise stepping out the waltz pattern in time to the song.

ASSESSMENT POINTS
Make a note of those children who:
• talk about the music with knowledge of the elements; • respond to metre-in-three (waltz steps); • sing with control of pitch and dynamics; • sing a descant.

MUSICAL ELEMENTS
Pitch; Duration; Tempo

SPECIFIC OBJECTIVES
■ Improvising a metre-in-three rhythm pattern ■ Improvising a waltz tune ■ Recognising intervals

KEY WORDS
Leap, interval

RESOURCES
■ CD 1 Track 1 'Inch Worm' ■ Non-pitched instruments ■ Pitched instruments with B♭/A# ■ Tape recorder

Composing A Slow Waltz

ACTIVITIES	WATCHPOINTS

■ *Finding intervals*

Ask the class to sit in a circle with a collection of instruments (pitched and non-pitched) in the middle. Play Track 1 and remind the class of how the melody leaps on the words 'Inch worm, Inch worm, measuring the marigolds'. Explain that the musical term for a 'leap' or 'step' is an 'interval'. Challenge individuals to find the 'Inch worm' intervals on pitched percussion, and to play them at the right time with the recording. **W1**

■ *Improvising*

Ask a small group of children to make up a slow metre-in-three rhythm pattern with non-pitched instruments. When this is secure, invite a volunteer to improvise a melody on top. Challenge them to include some leaps in the melody and to repeat short patterns or phrases. Give as many turns as time allows. **W2**

W1 *The pitches for these intervals are indicated on Photocopy sheet 2.*

W2 *You will probably find that it is the most confident children who volunteer and that they will need much encouragement and several attempts before they achieve a tune that they can remember and repeat. Be satisfied with modest attempts at first.*

FOLLOW UP
Divide the class into groups of about six and give them time to practise, first setting up a slow metre-in-three rhythm pattern and then an individual improvising a melody. Record each attempt and then spend time with the children evaluating their work. Did they keep a steady beat — metre-in-three? Did they play slowly? Did anyone manage to improvise a melody?

EXTENSION ACTIVITIES
Challenge those who learn instruments to use them for improvising their melodies and to find and include some 'Inch worm' intervals.

SUPPORT ACTIVITIES
Do not insist on the shy children improvising in front of the whole class. Work with them individually in a quiet space, playing a slow waltz beat for them while they experiment to find a melody.

ASSESSMENT POINTS
Make a note of those children who:
• recognise and can find the 'Inch worm' intervals; • can improvise a waltz rhythm; • can improvise a waltz tune.

Notin' Around

Shena Power

Section 1

Whole notes are strong.

Make them last long.

Section 2

Half notes fill the har - mo - ny, and

this tune fits in per - fect - ly.

Section 3

Quar - ter notes are bold and stead - y.

Walk - ing through this tune we've found that

If we sing it once through bright - ly,

we can sing it round and round.

Section 4

When you're in a hur-ry then the eighth notes are the best, be-cause they

simp-ly keep on run-ning and you nev-er take a rest, And you can

tra-vel up and down the scale with el-e-gance and ease, and if you

don't de-cide to stop in time you'll end up on your knees!

Section 5

It's sound ed-u-ca-tion— to add syn-co-pa-tion.— Just

swing in-to ac-tion— to jazz up— this song!

Sounds of Music

PS5

Dominoes

whole notes	half notes	quarter notes	eighth notes

MUSICAL ELEMENTS
Duration; Timbre; Texture; Structure

SPECIFIC OBJECTIVES
■ Singing a round in five parts   ■ Learning about music notation

KEY WORDS
Whole notes, half notes, quarter notes, eighth notes, coda

RESOURCES
■ CD 1 Tracks 3 and 4 'Notin' Around'   ■ Photocopy Sheets 3 and 4
■ Photocopy Sheet 5, photocopied 4 times and cut into 'dominoes'   ■
Pitched instruments (recorders/others played by the children)

Notin' Around

ACTIVITIES	WATCHPOINTS

■ *Listening and appraising* **W1**

Give out Photocopy sheets 3 and 4. Ask the class to follow the words and notation as they listen. Play Track 4 several times. Ask: How many sections are there? *(Five.)* What do you notice about the rhythm patterns in each section? *(Each section uses a different length note.)* **W2** What do you notice about the texture? *(It is sung through once in unison, and then builds up in layers.)* **W3**

■ *Learning about note values*

Divide the class into four groups (eight if the class is large) and give one set of the Photocopy sheet 5 'dominoes' to each group. Ask them to sort the dominoes (all whole notes together, all half notes etc.) and put them in the order in which they are used in the song.

Allocate each of the first four sections of the song to a group. Set up a steady beat (quarter notes) on a drum yourself, and help each group to tap out the rhythm of their section using non-pitched percussion instruments or body sounds. When they are confident, layer them group by group, signalling when each group should start and stop playing. Vary the order once the children become confident.

W1 *International note names are used here because they are easier to learn and understand, and more widely used than the idiosyncratic British terminology. Children who are already familiar with minims, crotchets, etc. through instrumental lessons will readily make the necessary connections.*

W2 *Whole notes ○ , half notes ♩ ♩, quarter notes ♩ ♩ ♩ ♩ , eighth notes ♫ ♫ ♫ ♫ and finally a jazzy pattern.*

W3 *The second time through, the singers are divided into five groups. Group 1 sings section 1, repeating it over and over again. Group 2 joins in with section 2, repeating it, and so on until all five sections are sung together, ending with an instrumental coda.*

FOLLOW UP
Put the most confident musicians into a fifth group, and help them learn the 'jazzy' section 5. Play Track 4 and ask each group to sing their section when it occurs. Pause and repeat until each group is very familiar with their part. Now sing the song unaccompanied and build it up in layers until all five lines are being sung together. Spend some time practising this and don't worry if a line breaks down. Allow the group to come in again when they feel confident. Finally, use Track 3 with the balance control to isolate the accompaniment, and perform the whole song with the recording.

EXTENSION ACTIVITIES
Allow small groups to select instruments and to practise ways of performing the lines together. Ask them to pay particular attention to the timbre of the ensemble. There should be a good balance between the various instruments.

SUPPORT ACTIVITIES
Make sure the least confident children have the simpler parts (quarter notes if you are playing a steady beat, or half notes).

ASSESSMENT POINTS
Make a note of those children who:
   • can layer rhythms confidently;   • understand simple note values;   • can sing in a five-part texture.

17

Name ....

Date ....

Are You Listening?
Concertos

You will hear two concertos. Listen carefully and circle the words which best describe the music you hear.

Johann Sebastian Bach **Brandenburg** **Concerto No. 4,** **Movement 1**	**Antonio Vivaldi** **The Four Seasons,** **Winter, Largo**
recorders	recorders
violin	violin
trumpet	trumpet
oboe	oboe
harpsichord	harpsichord
organ	organ
strings	strings
woodwind	woodwind
brass	brass
metre in 2	metre in 2
metre in 3	metre in 3
metre in 4	metre in 4
very slow	very slow
slow	slow
fast	fast
very fast	very fast
one melody	one melody
melodies weaving together	melodies weaving together
-----------------------------------	-----------------------------------
-----------------------------------	-----------------------------------
-----------------------------------	-----------------------------------

Add some words of your own to describe the music.

MUSICAL ELEMENTS

Timbre; Texture

SPECIFIC OBJECTIVES

■ Listening to identify texture and timbre   ■ Discussing the music and expressing opinions about it

KEY WORDS

Concerto Grosso, parts that weave

RESOURCES

■ CD 1 Track 5 Bach: *Brandenburg Concerto No 4*, Mvt 1 (extract); Track 6 Vivaldi: *The Four Seasons (Winter)*, Largo   ■ Photocopy Sheet 6
■ Poster 1

Concertos

ACTIVITIES

■ *Learning about the music*

Tell the children that they are going to hear music by two famous European composers: Johann Sebastian Bach (German, 1685–1750); and Antonio Vivaldi (Italian, 1678–1741). Both wrote music for dukes and princes who employed musicians to compose music and play for their courts. Solo parts were taken by the members of the orchestra and often there were two or three soloists. The composer's chief task was to make a contrast between the music played by the orchestra and by the soloists. A piece for solo and orchestra was a concerto. A concerto grosso (great concerto) was one where there were several soloists. **W1**

■ *Listening to two concerti*

Give out Photocopy sheet 6. Explain to the children that they will hear two extracts, both of which are for solo instruments and orchestra. The task is to listen and to identify the instruments playing and the expressive qualities of the music, circling the appropriate words on the sheet. Play Tracks 5 and 6, allowing at least one 'free listen' before the children write anything. Discuss the children's answers. **W2**

WATCHPOINTS

W1 *'Concerto' comes from the Italian 'concertare', meaning 'to compete'.*

W2 *Appropriate answers would be: Bach—solo recorders, solo violin, solo harpsichord, strings, woodwind, metre-in-three, fairly fast, melodies weaving together; Vivaldi—solo violin, pizzicato strings, metre-in-four, slow, one melody with accompaniment.*

FOLLOW UP

Make time during the week to listen to the music again and allow the children time to talk about it, using their own words to give their opinions. How does the music make them feel? What are the similarities between the pieces? What are the differences? How have composers made a contrast between soloists and orchestra? Use Poster 1 to aid discussion about melodies weaving together.

EXTENSION ACTIVITIES

Challenge more able children to research Bach or Vivaldi. What other music did they write? Encourage them to use the library or a CD ROM if there is one available.

SUPPORT ACTIVITIES

Give more reticent children the opportunity to talk with you individually about the music they have heard.

ASSESSMENT POINTS

Make a note of those children who:
  • can identify aspects of texture and timbre in their listening;   • express their opinions about music confidently.

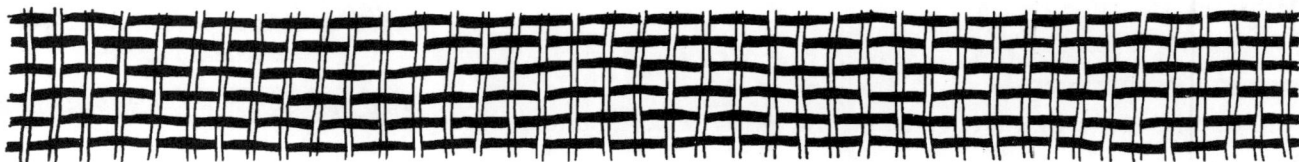

name _____

date _____

Weaving melodies

Action plan

1. Choose two pitched instruments.
2. Use pitches C D E G A.
3. Invent a question piece.
4. Next invent an answer piece.
5. Practise each piece.
6. Now play both pieces together.
7. Record your weaving melodies.
8. Listen to your weaving music. Use the checklist and make notes. Can you improve your piece?

Composing checklist

1. Is it the right length?
2. Is the combination of steps and leaps right?
3. Are there any repeated phrases?
4. Is the tempo right?
5. Are the dynamics right?
6. Have you chosen the right instruments?

MUSICAL ELEMENTS
Pitch; Texture; Structure

SPECIFIC OBJECTIVES
- Composing weaving melodies

KEY WORDS
Weaving melodies, drone, ostinato

RESOURCES
- Pitched instruments (C D E G A C' D' E' G') ■ Board or flip chart
- Photocopy Sheet 7 ■ Tape recorder ■ Poster 1

Weaving Melodies

ACTIVITIES

WATCHPOINTS

■ *Composing weaving melodies*

Sit the class in a circle. Invite an individual to invent a short melody (question), using the pitches listed above. Ask a second child to improvise a short answer on another instrument. Suggest they both start and finish on C or C'. When they can repeat their melodies, record them on the board either using letter names or quarter notes on a music staff. Now see if the two melodies can be played simultaneously. **W1**

It does not matter if one melody is longer than the other. Give several pairs of children the opportunity to work in this way and encourage them to extend their short melodies into longer ones as they grow in confidence.

Use Poster 1 and through discussion make the connection between the weaving lines in the pictures and the way in which melodies can weave together. **W2**

W1 *The five pitches C D E G A—high or low—form a pentatonic scale, and any melodies made from a pentatonic scale should sound good together.*

W2 *You may wish to link this with design & technology or art work.*

FOLLOW UP
Ask the children to work in pairs or small groups and to compose and record/notate their own weaving melodies, using Photocopy sheet 7.

EXTENSION ACTIVITIES
Some children may like to sing their melodies or play them on recorders or other instruments. They could also play a simple drone on pitched percussion or find a simple ostinato to accompany their melodies.

SUPPORT ACTIVITIES
For those children who find it difficult to weave their melodies together, let them keep them as 'question and answer'. They too could add a drone or melodic ostinato.

ASSESSMENT POINTS
Make a note of those children who:
- can compose a question/answer melody; • can compose an interweaving melody.

Silver Moon

Anon.

Moon, Moon, bright and shin - y moon, Won't you

Oh Sil - ver Moon, Moon, bright and shin - y moon, Won't you

please shine down on me?_____

please shine down on me?_____ Oh Sil - ver

Moon, Moon bright and shin - y moon Won't you

Moon, Moon, bright and shin - y moon, Won't you

come from be - hind that tree?

come from be - hind that tree? Oh, my

Hoo,

heart is bump - ing and I'm scared to see, There's a

hoo, Oh

creep - y sha - dow hang - ing ov - er me, Oh Sil - ver

Moon, Moon, bright and shin - y moon, Won't you

Moon, Moon, bright and shin - y moon, Won't you

please shine down on me?

please shine down on me?

Silver Moon

MUSICAL ELEMENTS

Pitch; Texture

SPECIFIC OBJECTIVES

■ Singing a song in two parts, with one part providing a descant

KEY WORDS

Descant

RESOURCES

■ CD 1 Tracks 7 and 8 'Silver Moon' ■ Photocopy Sheets 8 and 9
■ Non-pitched instruments ■ Poster 1

ACTIVITIES

WATCHPOINTS

■ *Listening to and appraising the song*

Play Track 8, focusing the children's listening with questions. Ask: How many vocal parts are there in verse 2? *(Two.)* Is the melody sung in the lower or upper part? *(Lower.)* What is the word used to describe the harmony part when it is higher than the melody? *(Descant.)* **W1**
Use Poster 1 to reinforce the concept of melodies weaving.

W1 *Use the balance control to highlight the melody (left) or descant (right).*

■ *Singing the song*

Use Track 8, turning the balance control to the left, to help the children learn the melody. When they are singing confidently with the recording, turn the balance control to the right and let them sing the melody against the descant on the recording. Reverse the process to learn the descant.

FOLLOW UP

When the children know both parts well, play Track 7 with the balance control turned to the right and divide the class into two groups to sing both parts together with the accompaniment. The song goes with a swing. It should be sung in a rhythmically relaxed manner, but the singers should sound as one voice. Remind the children to listen carefully to their neighbours' singing. Take care with the *'come from behind that'* phrase and don't rush it.

EXTENSION ACTIVITIES

Ask small groups of the more able singers and instrumentalists to choose some word patterns from the song to make a rhythm ostinato accompaniment (e.g. moon, moon, moon, moon; bright and shiny moon, bright and shiny moon; heart is bumping, heart is bumping). Have them play these patterns using non-pitched percussion instruments or body sounds as the rest of the class sings with the recording.

SUPPORT ACTIVITIES

Help the less confident singers to articulate the words rhythmically by asking them to whisper the words or to sing them on one pitch. Encourage them to exaggerate the beginnings and endings of the words.

ASSESSMENT POINTS

Make a note of those children who:
• can maintain an independent part against a descant; • can sing a descant; • can layer rhythms for an accompaniment; • articulate words clearly when singing.

Turn, Turn, Turn

Words from the Book of Ecclesiastes
Adaptation and music by Pete Seeger

Refrain

To ev - 'ry - thing (Turn, turn, turn,) There

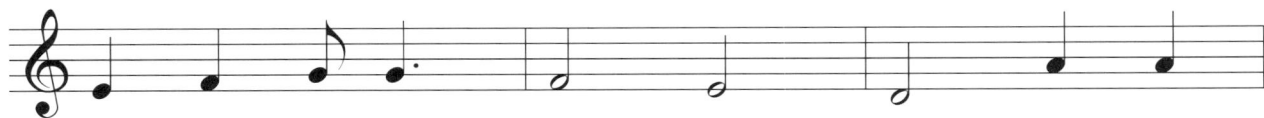

is a sea - son (Turn, turn, turn) And a

Fine
(last time only)

time for ev - 'ry pur - pose un - der heav - en.

Verse

1. A time to be born, a time— to die; A time to
2. A time to— gain, a time— to lose; A time to

plant, a time— to reap; A time to kill, a time— to
rend a time— to mend; A time to love, a time— to

heal; A time to laugh, a time to weep.—
hate; A time for peace, it's not too late.—

Turn, Turn, Turn
accompaniment

Verse

A time to be born, a time— to die, A time to plant, a time— to reap; A time to kill, A time— to heal; A time to laugh, a time to weep.—

MUSICAL ELEMENTS
Pitch; Timbre; Texture; Structure

SPECIFIC OBJECTIVES
■ Singing with control of pitch, dynamics and phrasing ■ Singing a verse in canon ■ Adding a counter-melody ■ Arranging a song for performance

KEY WORDS
Canon, verse and refrain

RESOURCES
■ CD 1 Tracks 9 and 10 'Turn, Turn' ■ Non-pitched and pitched instruments ■ Photocopy Sheets 10 and 11

Turn, Turn

ACTIVITIES	WATCHPOINTS
■ Singing the song Play Track 10. Explain that the music was composed by a famous American folk singer, Pete Seeger, and the words are taken from the Bible. Play the recording again and ask them what they notice about the structure of the song. Encourage them to identify the verse and refrain structure amongst their answers. Discuss their ideas. **W1** Ask the children to listen carefully to verse 2, and play Track 10 again. Help them to notice that the words and melody are sung in two parts, the second starting after the first and imitating it exactly. Explain that this is called a canon. **W2** **■ Singing in canon** Divide the class into two groups and practise singing verse 2 in canon. Then sing the whole song, dividing for the canon in verse 2.	**W1** *You may wish to give out Photocopy sheet 11.* **W2** *Turn the balance control to the left to focus on part 1 and to the right for part 2. For further work on singing in canon see Unit 4 Lesson 4.*

FOLLOW UP
Ask pairs of children to work out one of the accompaniment patterns on Photocopy sheet 10. Help them recognise when to play by clapping the patterns to the words as shown. Practise playing the accompaniment and singing the verse. As a class decide how this piece should be presented and performed, for instance at a class assembly. (A large group of pupils could sing the refrain each time; the verse could be sung by a small group or as solos; contrasting dynamics could be chosen for the refrain and verse.)

EXTENSION ACTIVITIES
Let volunteers sing solos and encourage those who learn instruments to play the accompaniments.

SUPPORT ACTIVITIES
Provide time for children to practise playing the accompaniments with the recording.

ASSESSMENT POINTS
Make a note of those children who:
•can sing in canon; • can play an accompaniment; • contribute ideas for an arrangement of the song for assembly; • sing a solo for assembly.

Assessment for Unit 1

Using some aspects of the checklist below you may identify what the children are able to do when they have followed Unit 1.

MUSICAL ACTIVITIES

PERFORMING:

- sing in canon;
- sing with control of pitch and dynamics;
- sing a descant;
- sing in a five-part texture;
- maintain an independent part against a descant;
- articulate words clearly when singing;
- sing a solo for assembly;
- play an accompaniment;
- play a waltz accompaniment;
- layer rhythms confidently.

COMPOSING:

- improvise a waltz rhythm;
- improvise a waltz tune;
- layer rhythms for an accompaniment;
- contribute ideas for an arrangement of a song for assembly;
- compose a question/answer melody;
- compose an interweaving melody.

LISTENING AND APPRAISING:

- talk about music with knowledge of the elements;
- identify aspects of texture, timbre and structure;
- express their opinions about music confidently;
- respond to metre-in-three through movement;
- recognise and find intervals;
- understand simple note values.

About Unit 2
Festivals of lights

Every year different people from different cultures, countries and religions celebrate with lights to brighten the darkest time of year. Hindus, throughout India and across the world, celebrate Divali by lighting lamps and fireworks. Many believe that it was the night when Lakshmi, the goddess of wealth, was saved from the King of the Demons. Some celebrate the victory of Rama over the evil Ravana. The story of Christmas tells of the birth of Jesus. The different Christian customs and traditions all include candles and bright lights and many make it an occasion for giving presents. Jewish people celebrate the festival of Chanukah. They too exchange gifts and light the candles of the menorah (nine branched candlestick).

The music in this unit will make a useful contribution to the children's multicultural education. The lessons can be used not only to achieve the musical learning objectives they address, but also to enhance understanding of different cultures and faiths. They extend the children's understanding of timbre, texture and structure particularly, and include some more focused composing activities.

Lessons
1 Polish The Old Menorah
2 Composing In Layers
3 Divali Song

4 Now Light 1000 Christmas Lights
5 Are You Listening? Christmas Music

TARGETS FOR UNIT 2

The following questions will help you identify what the children know, understand and can do, particularly focusing on how they talk about their music, express their opinions and apply their knowledge and understanding to their performing and composing work.

- How confidently do the children contribute ideas when discussing music?
- How well do the children evaluate their music?
- How effectively do they re-use ideas and apply new learning to composing and performing tasks?

Polish the Old Menorah

Words and music by Joan Arnold

Slow Refrain

Po - lish the old Me - no - rah,

Po - lish the old Me - no - rah,

Cha - nu - kah's here a - gain!

Cha - nu - kah's here a - gain!

Can - dles we light— one for each night.—

Can - dles we light one for each

Fine

Cha - nu - kah's here a - gain.

night here a - gain.

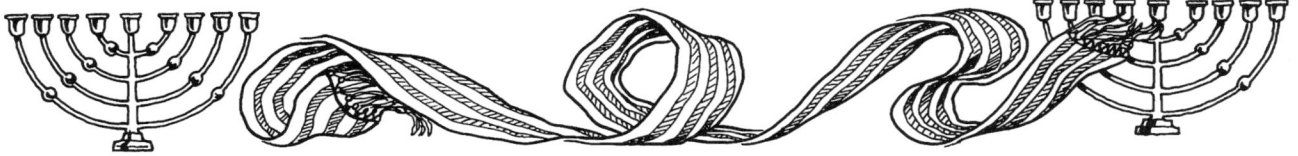

Much faster

Verse

1. Once u - pon a time there was war there was fight - ing.
2. When the war was o - ver they re - built the tem - ple.

Fight - ing for the tem - ple with sling and with sword.
This was then the mir - a - cle we ce - le - brate.

Ju - das Ma - ca - bee and his brave band of sol - diers
Sent a man a - way to fetch oil on his don - key

Fought a - gainst the Syr - ians in praise of the Lord.
And the one day's oil went on burn - ing for eight.

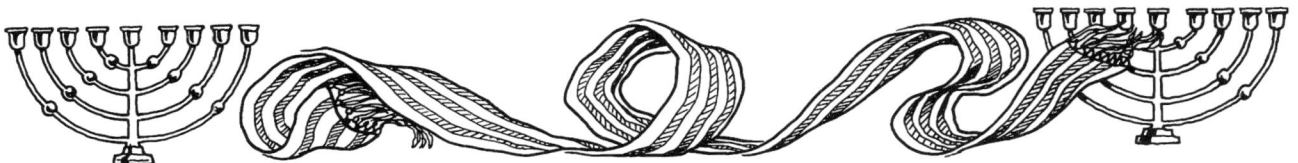

Name _____

Date _____

Are You Listening?
The elements

Tempo
At what speed is the song sung?

1. all slow

2. all fast

3. slow then fast

4. slow and fast alternately

Dynamics
How are the dynamics?

1. all quiet

2. all loud

3. quiet then loud

4. alternately quiet then louder

Texture
Describe the texture of the music.

1. unison line only

2. two voice parts only

3. one section in two parts and one section in unison

4. alternating between two parts and unison singing

Structure
How is this song structured?

1. one section (A)

2. two sections (AB)

3. three sections (ABA)

4. verse and refrain (ABABA)

MUSICAL ELEMENTS
Dynamics; Tempo; Texture; Structure

SPECIFIC OBJECTIVES
- Singing in two parts with control of tempo and dynamics
- Recognising unison and two part singing ■ Recognising verse/refrain structure ■ Learning how timbre, texture and dynamics affect style
- Inventing a rhythmic accompaniment

KEY WORDS
Menorah, Chanukah

RESOURCES
- CD 1 Tracks 11 and 12 'Polish the Old Menorah' ■ Non-pitched instruments ■ Photocopy Sheets 12, 13 and 14 ■ Poster 2

Polish The Old Menorah

ACTIVITIES

WATCHPOINTS

■ Listening and appraising
Go over the questions on Photocopy sheet 14 with the children. Explain that they will have three chances to listen to the song and decide before answering the questions. Play Track 12 three times and after the third listening, get them to circle their answers. Collect in the sheets and then discuss their answers with them and talk about the style of the music *(dynamics—alternately quiet then louder; tempo— slow and fast alternately; texture—alternating between two parts and a unison line; structure—verse and refrain)*. **W①**

■ Learning a song in two parts
Give out Photocopy sheets 12 and 13. Go over the words and recount the story of Chanukah. **W②**

Play Track 12 again, turning the balance control to the left to focus on the melody, and ask the children to join in. When they are familiar with the melody, turn the balance control to the right and let them sing it against the second, lower part. Reverse the process to learn the lower part.

W① *The written answers may give an indication of how well the children understand the elements of music, and how well they listen, but the discussion afterwards is the most important part of the activity.*

W② *The words of the song explain the story but if you have* Sounds of Music Year 2/P3, *there is another Chanukah song and more information. Explain that a menorah is the nine-branched candlestick traditionally used at Chanukah. It is sometimes known as a Chanukia, and is shown on Poster 2.*

FOLLOW UP
Divide the class into two groups, with some confident singers in each group. Use Track 11 and practise singing the song in two parts, gradually turning the balance control to the right to fade out the recorded voices as the children become more assured. Give them plenty of practice in singing the words of the refrain so they are clear and distinct, and help them slow down for the pause ⌢ at the end. Encourage them to make a contrast between the slower, quieter refrain and the lively verses.

EXTENSION ACTIVITIES
Challenge small groups of more able children to invent a simple repeated rhythm accompaniment using the pattern of some of the words (e.g. 'polish the old me-' and 'candles we light'). Have them play their rhythms as the class sings.

SUPPORT ACTIVITIES
Allow the less able children extra time to listen to the recording in order to complete their question sheets.

ASSESSMENT POINTS
Make a note of those children who:
- sing and maintain an individual part confidently; • recognise aspects of dynamics, tempo, texture and structure and discuss them with meaning; • can invent a rhythm accompaniment to word patterns.

Composing in layers

1. Mac - ca - bees   Mac - ca - bees   Ju - das Mac - ca - be - as

2. Swing - ing our   swords   and   us - ing slings and ar - rows

3. Ov - er - come the Sy - ri - ans,   save the ho - ly tem - ple

4. Vic - tor - y   is ours,   we'll light the tem - ple light

5. Not   much   oil.   It   won't   last

6. Bet - ter send a man to fetch some It will take eight days

7. Walk - ing   walk - ing   with   my   don - key

Questions for evaluating a performance

Did it start crisply? Did we keep in time? Were the words clear? Did we play too loudly? Did we finish together? Did it go as planned? How could we improve it?

MUSICAL ELEMENTS

All the elements

SPECIFIC OBJECTIVES

■ Performing a layered rhythm ostinato ■ Arranging a layered ostinato
■ Inventing melodic ostinato patterns using a pentatonic scale ■
Tape recording and evaluating a performance

KEY WORDS

Layered ostinato

RESOURCES

■ Photocopy Sheet 15 ■ Non-pitched instruments (one per child)
■ Pitched instruments ■ Tape recorder

Composing In Layers

ACTIVITIES

■ *Performing rhythm patterns*

Give out Photocopy sheet 15, read through each pattern, and help the
children to chant them slowly and rhythmically. Play a slow drum
beat as shown, to keep the steady beat. Practise each pattern until the
children are confident and can change from one to another.

Now give out the non-pitched instruments and ask the children to play
the rhythm patterns as they say the words. Practise playing both
quietly and loudly, but keep to the steady beat.

■ *Arranging and performing a layered ostinato*

Divide the class into four groups and get them to choose (or allocate)
one pattern each from Photocopy sheet 15. Give each group an
opportunity to practise chanting and playing their rhythm.

Now, starting with group 1, in turn add (layer) the patterns on top of
each other. **W1**

Practise performing the ostinato and record your efforts when the
children are confident.

WATCHPOINTS

W1 *Each group continues to repeat its
line until you signal everyone to stop.
This is called a layered ostinato.*

FOLLOW UP

Listen to your recording of the layered ostinato and discuss with the children how you could improve your
performance. Use the questions on Photocopy sheet 15 to help you. Talk about starting and finishing and about the
dynamics. Try different orders or all starting together. Allow the children to make the decisions.

EXTENSION ACTIVITIES

Using the pitches of the pentatonic scale (C D E G A), challenge the more confident children to compose repeating
melodies for the rhythm patterns. Ask them to write the letter names above the words on Photocopy sheet 15 and
to play their melodies as they chant. Challenge them to layer their melodies together in twos, threes or fours.

SUPPORT ACTIVITIES

Allow everyone the opportunity of composing repeating melody patterns to the words. Give extra time and help to
the less confident children, and do not insist that they layer their melodies.

ASSESSMENT POINTS

Make a note of those children who:
  • can play a rhythm pattern as part of a layered ostinato; • can evaluate their performance; • invent melodic
  ostinati; • arrange a layered ostinato.

Divali Song

George Odam

Call *phrase A*   **Response** *phrase B*

Where the lights are twink - ling,   Brave Prince Ra - ma comes.

Call   **Response**

Can - dles by the hou - ses,   Prin - cess Si - ta comes.

Call *phrase C*   **Response**

From the dark - ness   Brave Prince Ra - ma comes.

Call   **Response**

In - to bright - ness   Prin - cess Si - ta comes.

MUSICAL ELEMENTS

Pitch; Duration; Structure

SPECIFIC OBJECTIVES

- Discovering and performing the melody by ear and from notation
- Understanding the structure of the melody ■ Composing over a drone using Rāg Bhairav

KEY WORDS

Phrase, call, response, Rāg Bhairav, drone

RESOURCES

- CD 1 Tracks 13 and 14 ■ Photocopy Sheets 16 and 17 ■ Pitched and non-pitched instruments ■ Poster 2 ■ Flipchart or board

Divali Song

ACTIVITIES

■ *Listening to and singing the song*

Sit the children in a circle. Play Track 14 several times and ask the children to hum with the melody as they pick it up. Explain that there are some phrases which appear more than once, with different words. Ask: How many different melodic phrases are there? *(Three.)* **W❶**

Help them to recognise the structure of the melody by asking which two phrases appear twice *(phrases A and C)* and which phrase occurs four times *(phrase B).* **W❷**

They will notice that phrase B is a response, sung by children, while phrases A and C are calls, sung by a solo woman. Encourage the class to sing the response, using Track 14 and turning the balance control to the right. Reverse the process to sing the call. Discuss Divali, using Poster 2. **W❸**

■ *Discovering the melody*

Make a xylophone or chime bars (pitches D to C') available in the centre of the circle. Sing through the song with the recording again and ask a volunteer to find phrase A ('Where the lights are twinkling'). Do the same for the other phrases. Listen again and ask the children to order the phrases as they appear in the song (A B A B C B C B). Write this on the board. Now ask for volunteers to play the whole melody. **W❹**

WATCHPOINTS

W❶ *The different phrases are marked on Photocopy sheet 16, but do not give out copies yet. It is important for the children to work out the structure by listening, without visual clues.*

W❷ *The children can identify the phrases by referring to the lyrics, e.g. 'Where the lights are twinkling' is the same as 'Candles by the houses'.*

W❸ *See page 29 for a little more information about Divali.*

W❹ *This can be done by individual children or groups of three, preferably with an instrument each, each playing one of the phrases each time it appears.*

FOLLOW UP

During the week, allow everyone an opportunity to practise playing the melody.

EXTENSION ACTIVITIES

Ask those who learn the melody to play it from the notation on Photocopy sheet 16. Then, in pairs and using Photocopy sheet 17, challenge one child to set up a drone while the other makes up a melody with repeated phrases using the pitches of Rāg Bhairav.

SUPPORT ACTIVITIES

Some children will need to practise the individual Divali Song phrases and may need to remain in groups of three to play the whole song.

ASSESSMENT POINTS

Make a note of those children who:
- recognise and can identify the structure of the melody; • can discover and perform the melody by ear; • can play the melody from notation; • can compose a melody over a drone.

Name _____ Date _____

Rāg Bhairav

These pitches make up Rāg Bhairav.

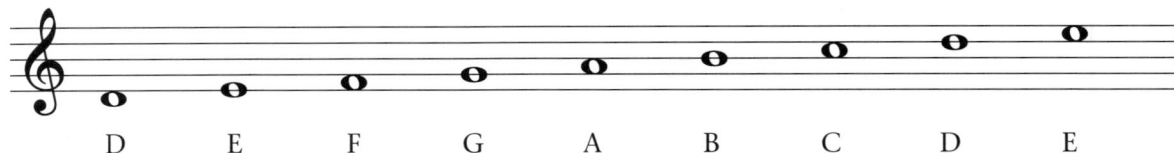

D E F G A B C D E

These are phrases A, B and C from Divali Song.
Use them to make up your melody, or invent your own patterns.

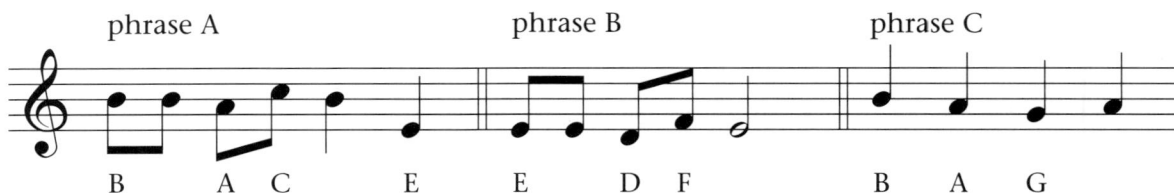

phrase A   phrase B   phrase C

B A C   E E D F   B A G

Make up a drone using pitches E and B. Vary the rhythm if you like.
Here are two ideas.

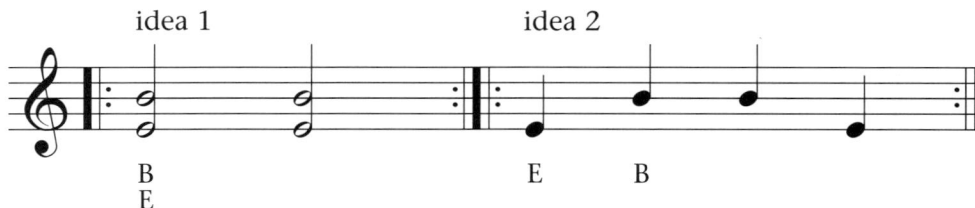

idea 1   idea 2

B
E   E B

Challenge: notate your melody on paper.

Now Light
One Thousand Christmas Lights

Folk song from Sweden

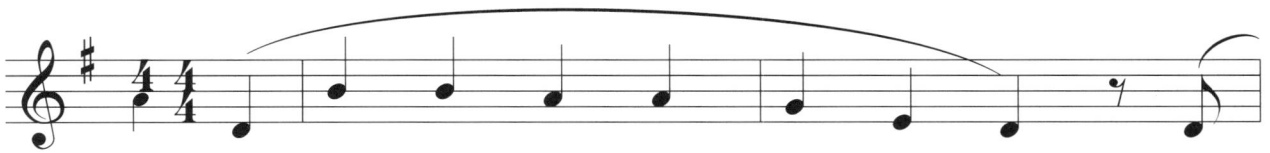

1. Now light one thou - sand Christ - mas lights, On
2. Oh once when skies were star - ry bright, In

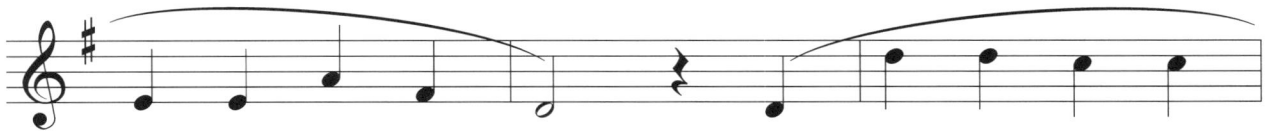

dark earth here to - night; One thou - sand thou - sand
sta - ble cold and bare, Sweet Ma - ry bore a

Verse 1

al - so shine To make the dark sky bright.
son that night, A

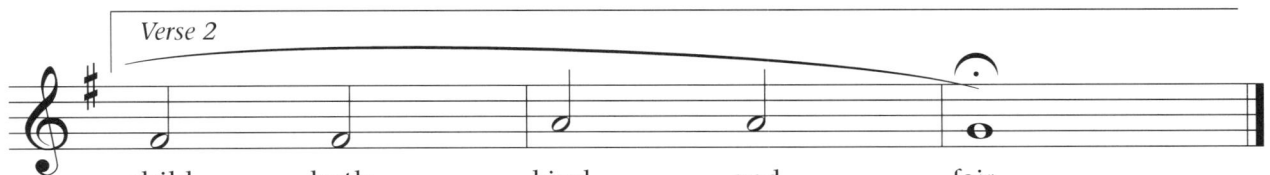

Verse 2

child both kind and fair.

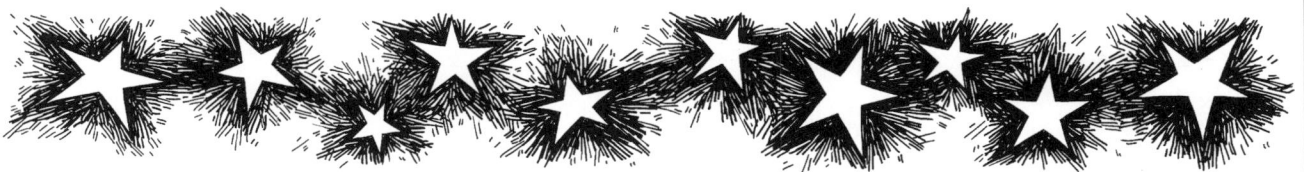

Now Light 1000 Christmas Lights

MUSICAL ELEMENTS
Duration; Timbre; Structure

SPECIFIC OBJECTIVES
■ Singing with attention to pitch, tone quality and breath control
■ Recognising a change in rhythm ■ Learning about rests

KEY WORDS
Augmentation

RESOURCES
■ CD 1 Track 15 'Now Light One Thousand Christmas Lights'
■ Photocopy Sheet 18 ■ Poster 2

ACTIVITIES

■ *Singing the song*

Play Track 15 several times for the children to pick up the song. They will soon be able to join in. **W1**

Ensure that the children sit in a relaxed but upright position and sometimes ask them to stand when they sing. Make sure they articulate the words clearly and take enough breath before each phrase to produce a focused, unbreathy sound. **W2**

■ *Listening to the rhythm*

When they know the song ask the children to compare the rhythm of the final phrase in the two verses and tell you what happens. *(In verse 2 the notes are doubled in length to make a slower ending—quarter notes (crotchets) become half notes (minims) and the final note is a whole note (semi-breve) instead of a half note (minim).)* **W3**

WATCHPOINTS

W1 *Focus the listening with a question each time. What is the song about? (Christmas lights, stars, Nativity.) You may wish to use Poster 2. What timbres can you hear? (Children and men's voices, bells, flute, guitar, percussion.) What is the metre of the song? (Metre-in-two.) What is the structure? (Introduction, verse 1, instrumental link, verse 2, coda.)*

W2 *This is a relatively simple song to learn so it is a good opportunity to concentrate on performance detail.*

W3 *The technical word for doubling the length of a note or notes is 'augmentation'. The children do not have to know this but may enjoy using a technical music term. Unit 1 Lesson 3 focuses on note names, and they are explained in the glossary.*

FOLLOW UP
Give out Photocopy sheet 18 and ask the class to follow the music while they sing. Ask: Where do you naturally take a breath? *(At the end of each phrase.)* What do you notice about the notation when you take a breath? *(There is a 'rest' or silence.)* Draw attention to the two rest symbols (𝄽 *quarter note;* 𝄾 *eighth note*). Refer back to Photocopy sheet 18 and ask the children to find some of the same rests.

EXTENSION ACTIVITIES
Ask for volunteers to sing a solo verse and challenge them to sing the verse in two breaths only, concentrating on a smooth and gentle line.

SUPPORT ACTIVITIES
Encourage less confident children to sing with a partner or in a small group.

ASSESSMENT POINTS
Make a note of those children who:
• sing with accurate pitch; • produce good tone quality; • sing with good breath control; • recognise a change in rhythm; • recognise and understand simple rests.

MUSICAL ELEMENTS
Timbre; Texture; Structure

SPECIFIC OBJECTIVES
■ Appraising a range of Christmas music ■ Comparing two arrangements of a melody ■ Identifying aspects of texture and timbre ■ Using appropriate language to describe music

KEY WORDS
Choir, vocal, instrumental, continuous, arrangement

RESOURCES
■ CD 1 Track 16 'In Dulci Jubilo'; Track 17 Bach: *Chorale Prelude*; Track 18 'O Come All Ye Faithful'; Track 19 Hely Hutchinson: *Carol Symphony*, Mvt 1 (extract) ■ Photocopy Sheets 19 and 20

Are You Listening?
Christmas music

ACTIVITIES

■ *Listening, appraising and comparing*
Give out Photocopy sheet 19 and explain that the class will hear two arrangements of the Christmas song 'In Dulci Jubilo'. The task is to choose words from the appropriate column on Photocopy sheet 19 to describe each arrangement. Ask them to circle the words they choose, but not until they have listened to each version twice. Play Tracks 16 and 17. Collect in the sheets and discuss their findings, focusing on the similarities and differences between the two pieces. **W1**
Appropriate answers would be:
Track 16: vocal, choir, solo, several verses, words, melody easy to hear.
Track 17: instrumental, organ, solo, continuous, no words, melody sometimes hidden.

WATCHPOINTS

W1 *Completing the sheets will focus children's listening, and may give you some idea of how well they understand what they hear, but the most important part is the discussion afterwards.*

FOLLOW UP
Repeat the listening activity using Photocopy sheet 20 and Tracks 18 and 19.
Appropriate answers would be:
Track 18: vocal, instrumental, band, organ, choir, several verses, words, melody easy to hear.
Track 19: instrumental, orchestra, continuous music, no words, melody sometimes hidden.

EXTENSION ACTIVITIES
Ask the more literate children to write a description of one of the pieces of music in their own words, and to say how the music makes them feel.

SUPPORT ACTIVITIES
Help the less literate to think of words to describe the music they have heard and how it makes them feel.

ASSESSMENT POINTS
Make a note of those children who:
• make appropriate comments about the music they have heard; • compare with understanding two arrangements of a Christmas melody; • can identify aspects of texture and timbre; • use language imaginatively to describe music.

Sounds of MUSIC

Name _____

Date _____

Are you listening?
In Dulci Jubilo

Listen to two arrangements of a piece of Christmas music.
Choose the words which best describe each arrangement.

In Dulci Jubilo	Bach: Chorale Prelude In Dulci Jubilo
vocal	vocal
instrumental	instrumental
band	band
orchestra	orchestra
organ	organ
choir	choir
solo	solo
several verses	several verses
continuous music	continuous music
words	words
no words	no words
melody easy to hear	melody easy to hear
melody sometimes hidden	melody sometimes hidden

Can you think of other words to describe this music?

Name

Date

Are you listening?
O Come, All Ye Faithful

Listen to two arrangements of a piece of Christmas music.
Choose the words which best describe each arrangement.

O Come, All Ye Faithful	Hely Hutchinson: Carol Symphony, Movement 1
vocal	vocal
instrumental	instrumental
band	band
orchestra	orchestra
organ	organ
choir	choir
solo	solo
several verses	several verses
continuous music	continuous music
words	words
no words	no words
melody easy to hear	melody easy to hear
melody sometimes hidden	melody sometimes hidden

Can you think of other words to describe this music?

Mistletoe and Wine

Words by Leslie Stewart and Jeremy Paul
Music by Keith Strachan

1. The child is a king, the carollers sing,
The old is past, there's a new beginning.
Dreams of Santa, dreams of snow,
Fingers numb, faces aglow. It's…

Refrain

Christ - mas time, mis - tle - toe and wine,

Child - ren sing - ing Chris - ti - an rhyme With

logs on the fire—— and gifts on the tree; A

(⌢ last time)

time to re - joice in the good that we see.

2. A time for living, a time for believing,
A time for trusting, not deceiving.
Love and laughter and joy ever after;
Ours for the taking, just follow the master.

3. It's a time for giving, a time for getting,
A time for forgiving, and for forgetting.
Christmas is love, Christmas is peace;
A time for hating and fighting to cease.

MUSICAL ELEMENTS
Duration; Timbre; Texture

SPECIFIC OBJECTIVES
- Singing with attention to pitch, tone quality and breath control
- Singing a solo ■ Listening for and discussing timbre and texture
- Composing a rhythm accompaniment (metre-in-three)

KEY WORDS
Glockenspiel

RESOURCES
- CD 1 Tracks 20 and 21 'Mistletoe and Wine' ■ Non-pitched instruments ■ Photocopy Sheet 21

Mistletoe And Wine

ACTIVITIES

■ *Singing the song* **W1**

Help the children to learn the song by playing Track 21 several times. Some may know it already. Ask them to concentrate on the refrain and to join in as soon as they feel confident. Encourage good posture, tone and breath control. **W2**

When they know the song, invite individuals or small groups to take on the solo verses, while the rest of the class sing the refrain. **W3**

■ *Discussing texture and timbre*

Initiate a discussion about the song. Talk about the texture (solo voice in the verses contrasting with many voices in the chorus) and the different timbres (bell-like glockenspiel sounds in the accompaniment). Ask: How does it create a Christmassy atmosphere? *(The lyrics, happy feeling, catchy melody, bells.)* **W4**

WATCHPOINTS

W1 *Use Track 21 with the balance control turned to the left to remove the solo man's voice; turn the balance control to the right to remove the children's voices. Use Track 20 with the balance control turned to the right to remove all the recorded voices.*

W2 *Refer back to Unit 2 Lesson 4 for hints about singing techniques.*

W3 *You may wish to give out Photocopy sheet 21.*

W4 *There are no right answers. This is a chance for the children to talk about what they hear and express opinions. Praise any that pick out musical features.*

FOLLOW UP
Ask the children to sway to the strong beat and see if they can identify metre-in-three. Using body sounds (claps, clicks, taps, etc.) ask them individually to create a pattern to accompany the song. Play the recording again and ask them to try their patterns quietly. Next ask them to perform their patterns to a partner and to refine them if they can.

EXTENSION ACTIVITIES
Ask those pairs who invent effective accompanying patterns to translate them onto non-pitched percussion and play them to the class with the recording.

SUPPORT ACTIVITIES
Gather the less rhythmically secure children together and give them further help with their metre-in-three accompaniments. Play the strong first beat of every three on a tambourine or drum and pick out one or two good ideas to practise all together.

ASSESSMENT POINTS
Make a note of those children who:
- • sing with accurate pitch; • sing producing good tone quality; • sing with good breath control; • sing a solo confidently; • can discuss timbre and texture; • can compose an effective rhythm accompaniment (metre-in-three); • can arrange a rhythm accompaniment on non-pitched percussion.

Assessment for Unit 2

Using some aspects of the checklist below you may identify what the children are able to do when they have followed Unit 2.

MUSICAL ACTIVITIES

PERFORMING:

- sing and maintain an individual part confidently;
- sing with accurate pitch;
- sing producing good tone quality;
- sing with good breath control;
- play a rhythm pattern as part of a layered ostinato;
- play a melody by ear;
- play a melody from notation.

COMPOSING:

- invent a rhythm accompaniment to word patterns;
- compose an effective rhythm accompaniment (metre-in-three);
- arrange a rhythm accompaniment on non-pitched percussion;
- invent melodic ostinati;
- arrange a layered ostinato;
- compose a melody over a drone.

LISTENING AND APPRAISING:

- recognise/identify aspects of dynamics, tempo, timbre, texture and structure and discuss them;
- evaluate their performance;
- recognise and identify the structure of a melody;
- discover a melody by ear;
- recognise a change in rhythm;
- recognise and understand simple rests;
- make appropriate comments about the music they have heard;
- use language imaginatively to describe music;
- compare with understanding two arrangements of a melody.

About Unit 3
The American influence

Much American music has its roots in the history of slavery and the chain gangs, and many songs also centre on the railroad, an important symbol of the opening up and development of North America. The railroad was more than just a means of transport; it meant freedom, opportunity, adventure and sometimes wealth. It also provided a means of escape for criminals and prisoners, like the composers of 'Rock Island Line' and 'Midnight Special', who dreamed of making their way by train to freedom. Other songs and music originate from the Hillbillies, Southern mountain dwellers who adapted their folk tradition to the city style, as in 'Worried man'. 'Heal the Soul' combines a traditional Native American chant with contemporary sounds, a mixture which achieved considerable popularity in the mid-1990s.

In this unit, children have the opportunity to listen to and discuss a range of music, and to learn about the American culture leading to jazz and the blues. Style and mood are considered, and the children are challenged to sing part songs, with attention to breath control and proper articulation of words.

Lessons

1 Simple Gifts	4 Heal the Soul	6 Songs of the West
2 Porgy and Bess	5 You'll Never Walk Alone	7 Making a Blues Song
3 The Blues		

TARGETS FOR UNIT 3

The following questions will help you to identify what the children know, understand and can do:

- How well do the children display their musical knowledge in class discussion?
- How well do the children control their singing through their control of breathing, dynamics and expression?
- How well do children demonstrate an understanding of style in their composing?

Simple Gifts

Traditional Shaker song

'Tis the gift to be sim - ple, 'tis the gift to be free, 'Tis the

gift to come down where you ought to be, And

when we find our - selves in the place just right, It - 'll

be in the val - ley of love and de - light.

When true sim - pli - ci - ty is gained, To

bow and to bend we shan't be a - shamed, To

turn, turn will be our de - light, Till by

turn - ing, turn - ing we come out right.

Simple Gifts accompaniments

Simple Gifts

MUSICAL ELEMENTS
Pitch; Duration; Dynamics; Tempo; Timbre; Texture; Structure

SPECIFIC OBJECTIVES
■ Devising dance movements to a song ■ Singing expressively and with breath control ■ Listening to and comparing music
■ Accompanying a song with instruments

KEY WORDS
Mood

RESOURCES
■ CD 2 Track 1 'Simple Gifts'; Track 2 Copland: *Appalachian Spring* (extract) ■ Pitched instruments, including any learned by the children
■ Space for movement ■ Poster 3 ■ Photocopy Sheets 22 and 23

ACTIVITIES

■ *Listening and responding to the song* **W1**
Introduce the Shakers, using Poster 3, which shows a room in a Shaker house. Notice that the furniture can be hung on pegs around the walls to give room for dancing. **W2**

In pairs or individually, ask the children to devise their own dance movements as they listen to Track 1. Encourage them to reflect the tempo and mood of the recording.

■ *Singing the song*
Encourage the children to join in with the recording when they can. Breathe where indicated (') on Photocopy sheet 22.

■ *Appraising Appalachian Spring* **W3**
Play Track 2 a number of times, focusing the listening with questions. Ask: How many times can you hear all or part of the 'Simple Gifts' melody? *(Seven.)* How does the melody change in character and mood? *(Bright and lively; melancholy.)* Which timbres are prominent? *(See below.)* Is the tempo always the same? *(No.)* Ask the children to listen for the time when the melody catches its tail, beginning again before the previous version has finished. **W4**

The order of events is: **1** violins, slow; **2** clarinet, thin accompaniment; **3** oboe and bassoon, thicker accompaniment; **4** low strings, smooth; **5** high and low strings weaving, 'catching tail'; **6** trumpet with other brass instruments, fanfare style; **7** clarinet and bassoon, quieter.

WATCHPOINTS

W1 *This tune may be familiar as a modern hymn, 'Lord of the Dance'.*
W2 *The Shakers were a religious group who lived in New England in the 18th century. They lived a simple, pious life according to strict rules. The nickname 'Shakers' comes from their belief that they could 'shake out evil' by dancing.*

W3 Appalachian Spring *was written for a 1944 ballet about a 19th century pioneer couple. Aaron Copland (1900–1990) was a famous American composer who often used folk tunes in his music.*

W4 *Use the pause button as you think necessary.*

FOLLOW UP
Divide the class into groups of four to six children. Give out Photocopy sheet 23 and allocate one part to each group. Help each group to identify the pitch and rhythm, giving them time to practise.
Gather the class together and combine the parts, one by one. See if the children can sing as they play, or ask one group to sing Simple Gifts while others play.

EXTENSION ACTIVITIES
Challenge instrumentalists to find the melody. Ask them to play it with the accompaniments.

SUPPORT ACTIVITIES
Make sure that less confident children play pattern 1 first and do not insist that they sing.

ASSESSMENT POINTS
Make a note of those children who:
• sing with good breath control; • devise appropriate movements; • can play a simple accompaniment; • can find and play the melody of the song; • listen with concentration; • discuss the music appropriately.

MUSICAL ELEMENTS
Timbre

SPECIFIC OBJECTIVES
■ Identifying soprano and bass voices ■ Identifying harp and soprano saxophone ■ Discussing music by Gershwin ■ Exploring contrasting moods

KEY WORDS
Soprano, bass, Gershwin, Porgy and Bess, opera, mood

RESOURCES
■ CD 2 Track 3 'Summertime'; Track 4 'I've Got Plenty of Nothin''; Track 5 Gershwin: *Porgy and Bess—A Symphonic Picture* (extract)

ACTIVITIES	WATCHPOINTS

■ *Listening to songs from Porgy and Bess*

Play through Tracks 3 and 4 and ask the children to decide how they might describe the mood of these two songs. Allow them to make notes as they listen. **W❶**

Lead a class discussion about the contrast between the songs. There will be many ideas but the main contrasts are in tempo and mood. *('Summertime' is a lazy, slow lullaby and 'I've got Plenty of Nothin'' is faster, bouncy and happy.)* Encourage the children to talk about the two voices. Ask: What is a high voice called? *(Soprano—'Summertime'.)* What is a low voice called? *(Bass—'I've got plenty of nothin''.)*

Explain that the songs come from an opera by George Gershwin (1898–1937), an American composer who was known for his jazzy style. Make sure the children know what an opera is (a story set to music and sung, accompanied by an orchestra) and tell them about Porgy and Bess. **W❷**

W❶ *You may need to play the songs several times.*

W❷ Porgy and Bess *was the first opera to be written for an all black cast. It is set on the waterfront (Catfish Row) in Charleston, South Carolina. Porgy is a disabled beggar, who rides on a goat-cart and who takes care of Bess. Bess has been deserted by her man, Crown, who killed a man in a fight over a card game. 'Summertime' is a lullaby sung to her baby by Clara, a fisherman's wife, at the beginning of the opera, and Porgy sings 'I've got plenty of nothin'' when he realises that Bess loves him.*

FOLLOW UP
Play Track 5, which is an orchestral version of the two songs. Once again, ask the class to make a note of the things they hear. In 'Summertime', ask: Which instruments play the melody? *(Violins, then soprano saxophone.)* Which instrument suggests shimmering heat? *(The harp.)* In 'I've got plenty of nothin'', ask: Which instruments play the melody? *(First banjo, then piccolo joins in, rich strings take over, banjo again, then brass and violins weaving together.)* How does Gershwin try to tell us this is Porgy's song? *(The trotting rhythms imitate the sound of his goat cart.)* Encourage the children to talk about the music and give them credit for expressing their own ideas and views.

EXTENSION ACTIVITIES
Challenge the more able children to find out more about Gershwin and his music from library books or a CD ROM.

SUPPORT ACTIVITIES
Make time for discussion with those who do not find it easy to express their ideas orally, and help them to identify the main features of the music.

ASSESSMENT POINTS
Make a note of those children who:
• can identify soprano and bass voices; • can identify harp, soprano saxophone, banjo, strings; • can talk about contrasting moods; • discuss music by Gershwin, using appropriate language.

51

Workaday Mornin' Blues

Music by Sol Berkowitz
Words by Rosemary Jacques

1. I'm weary of risin' at break of day,
   And havin' my chores to do,
   I'm weary of risin' at break of day,
   And havin' my chores to do,
   'Cause I've got me those work-a-day mornin' blues.

2. I'd rather go fishin' or spend my time
   Just dreamin' the whole day through,
   I'd rather go fishin' or spend my time
   Just dreamin' the whole day through,
   'Cause I've got me those work-a-day mornin' blues

3. But the bread in my pocket is mighty nice,
   It buys me some nice things too,
   The bread in my pocket is mighty nice,
   It buys me some nice things too.
   Got to chase away those work-a-day mornin' blues.
   Got to chase away those work-a-day mornin' blues.
   Work-a-day blues.

MUSICAL ELEMENTS
Pitch; Duration; Texture

SPECIFIC OBJECTIVES
■ Improvising a rhythmic accompaniment ■ Singing the blues with expression and style ■ Learning about some of the characteristics of blues

KEY WORDS
Blues

RESOURCES
■ CD 2 Track 6 'Work-a-day Mornin' Blues ■ Photocopy Sheet 24
■ Poster 3 ■ Non-pitched instruments ■ Drum and wire brushes (optional)

The Blues

ACTIVITIES

WATCHPOINTS

■ *Learning about the blues*

Play Track 6, and ask the children to explain what kind of feeling this music gives. Explain that Blues are sad songs about everyday living and that the expression 'feeling blue' means feeling sad. Link this with the history of the slave population of the USA in the last century. **W1**

Find the blues musicians on Poster 3 and discuss the instruments they have.

■ *Singing the blues and feeling the beat*

Sit the class in a circle and play the recording to them again, using the pause button to help them to learn the song phrase by phrase. Help them to feel the beat as strongly as they can by moving as they sit. Ask them to brush one hand across one knee on the first beat of the bar and to tap the other knee on the second beat. **W2**

Encourage them to perform this rhythm as they sing with the recording. Remind them to sing expressively.

W1 *Blues music came from African roots and expressed the misery of slavery on the colonial plantations. Even when slavery was abolished the traditions continued and gradually formed into jazz, rhythm and blues, and rock music.*

W2 *This should make a kind of brushing sound similar to the effect of the brushes on a drum. If you have some wire brushes, demonstrate a 'brush, tap' sound to the class.*

FOLLOW UP
Revise the 'brush, tap' movement with Track 6. Distribute a few non-pitched percussion instruments. Ask the children to play a 'brush, tap' pattern, very quietly, with the recording. Concentrate on quiet, controlled, rhythmic playing. Now, point to individual players and ask them to improvise their own jazzy patterns on top of the steady pulse that the class has set up. Give different children a chance to improvise in turn.

EXTENSION ACTIVITIES
Encourage able children to be more ambitious with their improvisations, listening carefully to the recording and trying to create more complicated patterns.

SUPPORT ACTIVITIES
Praise the less confident children if they manage to maintain the beat, and do not expect them to vary the pattern very much. Help them with one or two additional ideas.

ASSESSMENT POINTS
Make a note of those children who:
  • sing with expression and style; • maintain a steady beat; • can improvise a rhythmic pattern over a steady beat.

Are you listening?
Heal the Soul

a) What sound effects can you hear? How are the sound effects made?

b) What instrumental timbres can you hear?

c) Describe the singer's voice.

d) Can you hear repeated patterns?

e) What images do you think the composer wanted to conjure up? Do you think he was successful?

f) How does the music reflect the time when it was created? How does it reflect the place where it was created?

g) Listen to the contour of the vocal part, especially at the ends of phrases. Does it go mostly upward or mostly downward?

h) Why do you think the piece is called 'Heal the Soul'?

Native American music

Invent a piece in contemporary Native American style. Here are some hints.

1. Decide on the mood of the piece.

2. Invent some appropriate sound effects.

3. Choose two or three instrumental timbres.

4. Invent a melody pattern to play or sing. Use mostly D F G and A, and sometimes C. Begin and end on D.

5. Remember that Native American melodies go downwards at the end.

6. Decide how the piece will begin and end.

7. Find a way to record or write down your composition.

8. Can you think of ways to improve your piece?

MUSICAL ELEMENTS
All the elements

SPECIFIC OBJECTIVES
■ Composing in Native American style ■ Identifying traditional and contemporary features ■ Recognising how music reflects the time and place in which it is created ■ Listening to, appraising and learning about Native American music ■ Responding with language or art to the mood of the music

KEY WORDS
Contemporary, traditional, synthesized, mood, vocables, contour

RESOURCES
■ CD2 Track 7 'Heal the Soul' ■ Photocopy Sheet 25 ■ Pitched and non-pitched instruments ■ Tape recorder ■ Electronic keyboards/music software (optional) ■ Poster 3

Heal the Soul

ACTIVITIES

■ *Listening and appraising*

Use Poster 3 to remind children of the Native Americans who inhabited North America long before the European settlers arrived. **W1**

Explain that they will hear a piece of music, recorded recently by a Native American, which combines traditional and contemporary sounds. Play Track 7 several times, focusing the listening with the questions on Photocopy sheet 25. Acceptable answers may be:

a) sound effects, made on computer: birds, insects, wind

b) instrumental timbres: keyboard, strings

c) singer's voice: nasal, sliding

d) repeated patterns: keyboard phrase at the beginning, rhythm and melody patterns in the vocal part

e) images: perhaps open plains, loneliness, mystery

f) reflects time (synthesized sounds) and place (image of open plains)

g) vocal part contour: downward at the end of phrases **W2**

Explain that many Native American songs and chants use syllables with no fixed meaning, called 'vocables'. Discuss which features of the piece are traditional and which contemporary. (*Traditional: vocal timbre, downward contour, vocables. Contemporary: keyboard and string timbres, computer sound effects.*)

WATCHPOINTS

W1 *Children will be aware of the often negative images of Native Americans portrayed in films, particularly westerns and cartoons. Make sure they understand that today Native Americans live ordinary lives just like anyone else in the USA and Canada, although many live in towns in special reservations and are proud of their cultural heritage.*

W2 *This is characteristic of Native American music.*

FOLLOW UP
Divide the class into groups and set them the task of composing a short piece combining traditional Native American and contemporary features. Give out Photocopy sheet 25, or use it as a prompt. This is a good opportunity to use electronic keyboards or music software programs if you have them. Let the groups tape record their pieces, using the recordings to evaluate and refine their work.

SUPPORT ACTIVITIES
Help less confident children to invent sound effects and encourage individuals to improvise downward patterns. Give them the opportunity to use electronic keyboards or software if you can.

ASSESSMENT POINTS
Make a note of those children who:
- can compose, demonstrating understanding of style;   • can identify traditional and contemporary features;
- discuss the music they hear and compose, using appropriate language and demonstrating understanding of style;
- respond imaginatively with language or art to the mood of the music.

You'll Never Walk Alone

Words by Oscar Hammerstein II
Music by Richard Rodgers

When you walk through a storm, hold your head up high

And don't be a - fraid of the dark.

At the end of the storm is a gold - en sky

And the sweet sil - ver song of a lark.

Walk on through the wind, Walk on through the rain,

Though your dreams be tossed and blown,

crescendo poco a poco

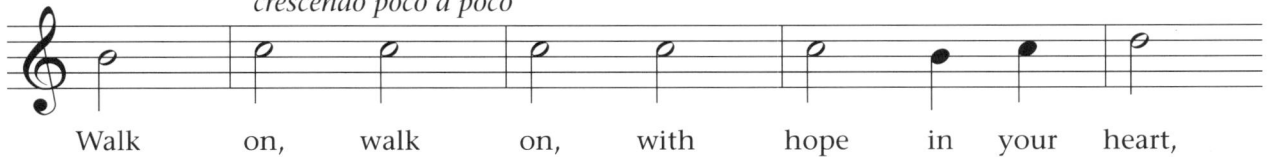

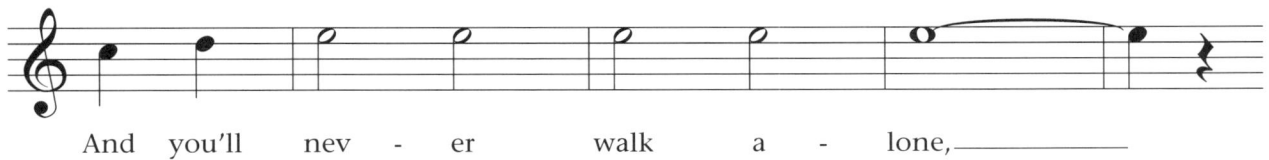

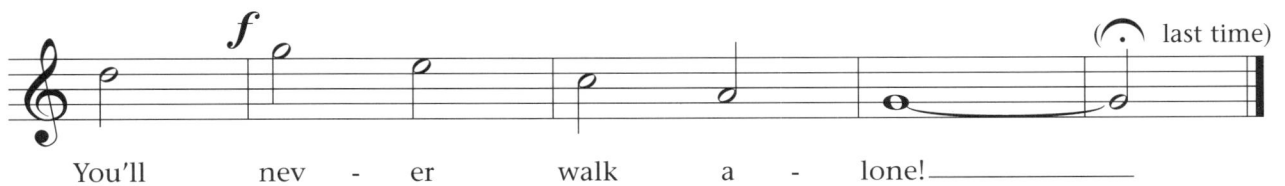

Walk on, walk on, with hope in your heart,

And you'll nev - er walk a - lone,

f

(last time)

You'll nev - er walk a - lone!

You'll Never Walk Alone

MUSICAL ELEMENTS

Pitch; Dynamics; Timbre; Structure

SPECIFIC OBJECTIVES

■ Developing breath control in singing ■ Singing with expression and in tune ■ Understanding Italian terms for dynamics

KEY WORDS

Dynamics

RESOURCES

■ CD 2 Track 8 'You'll Never Walk Alone' ■ Photocopy Sheets 26 and 27 ■ Poster 3

ACTIVITIES	WATCHPOINTS

■ *Listening and appraising*

Play Track 8 and ask the class if they have heard the song before. **W1**

Tell them that this song came originally from the stage and film musical *Carousel*, written in the USA by Richard Rodgers (music) and Oscar Hammerstein (words). Show Poster 3. The original story is partly a ghost story and tells of the continuing love, even after death, of a man for a woman. Focus the children's listening with questions. Ask: How does the melody begin? *(Quietly and low.)* How does it develop? *(Louder and higher in pitch until the climax of the song, with the highest pitches just before the end. This makes the song exciting as it grows.)*

■ *Singing the song*

Give out Photocopy sheets 26 and 27. Play the recording again and ask the children where would be the best places to breathe. Listening carefully to the recording should help them to decide. Ask them to mark the breathing places with a comma on their copies. This song needs to be sung with feeling and warmth. Ask the children to stand upright, feet slightly apart and in a relaxed pose, and at first to hum along with the recording. **W2**

When the children are clear about where to breathe, ask them to sing the words. As confidence grows concentrate on dynamics, first p *(p = piano = quiet)*, then mf *(mf = mezzo forte = moderately loud)* and crescendo poco a poco *(crescendo = getting louder, poco a poco = little by little)* up to f *(f = forte = loud)*. Help the children to identify the markings which show dynamics in the notation.

W1 *Today in Britain the song is associated with singing on the football terraces, and particularly with Liverpool FC.*

W2 *Standing helps breathing and avoids hunched up shoulders and squashed lungs. Think of being suspended by the top of the head in a line with your spine.*

FOLLOW UP

Practise the song as much as possible. Although it is quite difficult to sing it well, it is worth working on to obtain good, smoothly controlled singing and unanimity. The children should imagine the highest pitches as coming from the middle of their foreheads. Encourage them to listen to and blend with each other, not forcing the highest notes but making the fullest, sweetest sound.

EXTENSION ACTIVITIES

Encourage confident singers to sing a solo.

SUPPORT ACTIVITIES

Give the less confident a chance to sing in a small group rather than on their own.

ASSESSMENT POINTS

Make a note of those children who:
- sing with control of breathing; • singing with expression; • understand technical terms for dynamics.

MUSICAL ELEMENTS

Pitch; Duration; Tempo; Texture; Structure

SPECIFIC OBJECTIVES

■ Learning about the songs of the American West ■ Singing in three parts ■ Inventing and performing a rhythm accompaniment ■ Inventing and performing a hand jive

KEY WORDS

Medley; hand jive

RESOURCES

■ CD 2 Tracks 9 and 10 'Songs of the West' medley ■ Non-pitched percussion ■ Photocopy Sheets 28, 29, 30, 31 and 32

Songs of the West

ACTIVITIES	WATCHPOINTS

■ *Listening to and learning about the songs*

Play Track 9 and ask the children how many different songs they hear. *(Three —'Rock Island Line', 'Midnight Special' and 'Worried Man'.)* Talk about how they link together to form one piece of music. **W1**

Discuss the meaning and origins of these three songs. **W2**

■ *Creating a hand jive*

Pick out the strong accompanying rhythm (long, short, short) **W3** and get the children to pat it on their knees (left, right, right). Ask the children to contribute ideas for a hand jive. Choose the best actions and sequence them into a routine with the children. Listen again and perform the jive as a class.

W1 *The term for this is a medley.*

W2 *The heroes of many American folk songs in the 1930s and 1940s were railroad men and hoboes (travelling workers). The railroad itself was an important symbol to Americans and was more than just a means of transport—it also meant freedom and opportunity. You may wish to hand out the Photocopy sheets listed above.*

W3 *Long = half note, short = quarter note.*

FOLLOW UP

Concentrate on each song in turn. Play Track 10 again to help the class become familiar with words and melody, and give out the appropriate photocopy sheets. Turn the balance control to the left to focus on the melody and ask the children to sing, paying particular attention to the articulation of the words. Encourage them to sing with expression and with a swing.

EXTENSION ACTIVITIES

Help a few more adventurous children to learn the harmony parts of 'Midnight Special' and the second (descant) part of 'Worried Man'. Use Track 10 and turn the balance control to the right to focus on these parts. Notice that the second part of the song 'Midnight Special' echoes almost exactly the main tune, whilst the third part is a descant. When the children are confident, see if they can sing all three parts with the recording. Eventually use Track 9 with the balance control turned to the right, isolating the accompaniment only to support a sung performance of all three parts.

SUPPORT ACTIVITIES

Help less able children to provide a rhythmic accompaniment on non-pitched percussion.

ASSESSMENT POINTS

Make a note of those children who:
  • talk about the songs of the American West; • sing confidently in three parts; • can invent and perform a rhythm accompaniment; • can invent and perform a hand jive.

Rock Island Line

Traditional
Arranged by Brian Ley

Swung

Refrain

Oh the Rock Is- land Line— is a migh- ty good road,— Well the

Rock Is- land Line— is the road to ride,— Oh the Rock Is- land Line— is a

migh- ty good road, If you want— to ride it, got to ride it like you find it, Get your

| 1st time | 2nd and 3rd times | Fine |

tick- et at the station on the Rock Is- land Line. Rock Is- land Line.

Verse

1. Train's com - in' down the track, run - nin' real well,
2. Train left St Lou - is at quar - ter to nine,

Ooh wah ooh wah

Blow - in' the whis - tle and ring - in' the bell.—
Got to Fort Worth— for din - ner time.—

ooh wah ooh wah

Midnight Special

Traditional arranged by Brian Ley

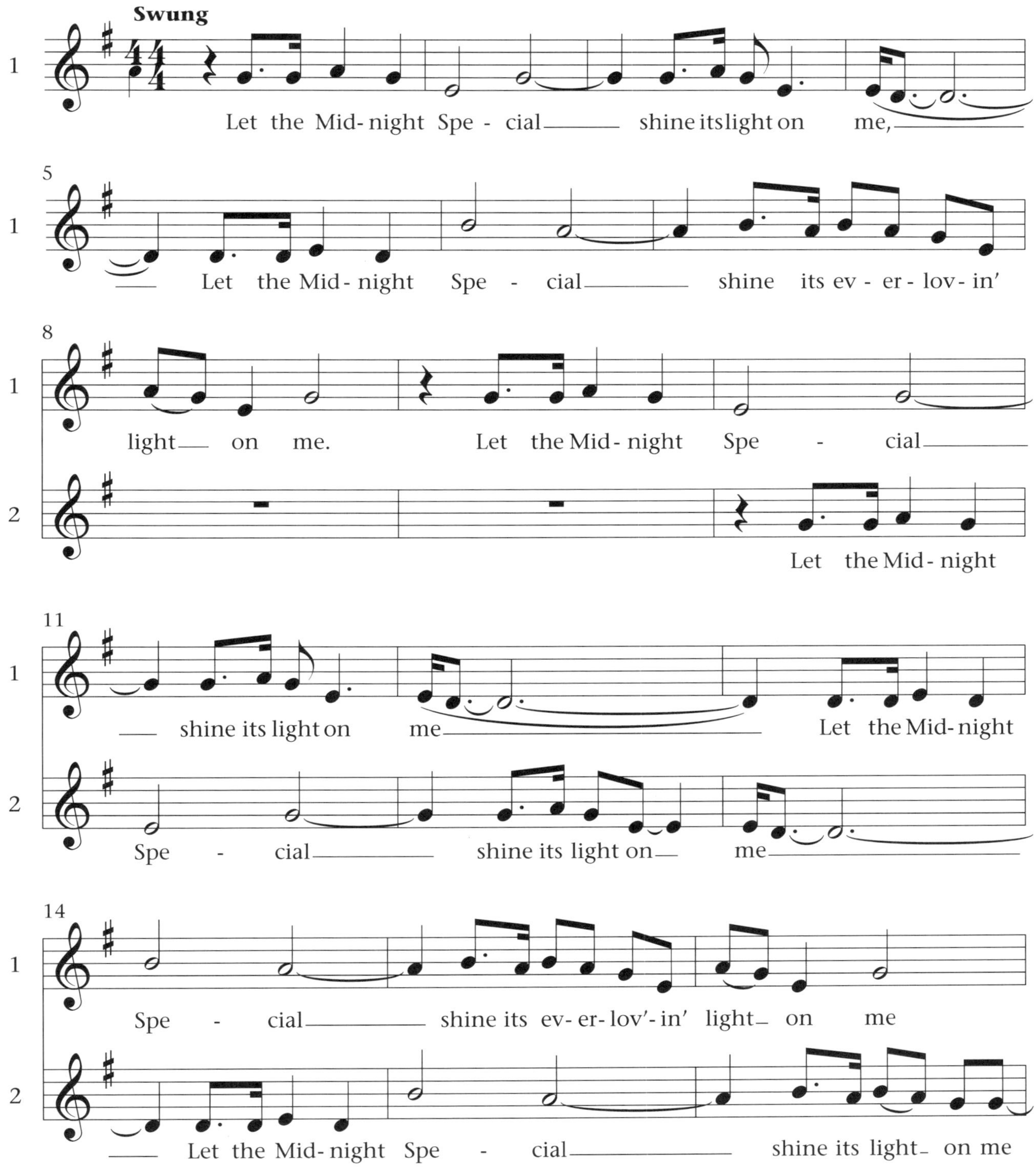

17
1
Let the Mid-night Spe - cial shine its light on
2
Let the Mid-night Spe - cial
3
Let the Mid-night Spe - cial shine its light on
20
1
me Let the Mid-night Spe - cial
2
shine its light on me Let the Mid-night
3
me Let the Mid-night Spe - cial
23
1
shine its ev - er - lov - in' light on me.
2
Spe - cial shine its light on me.
3
shine its ev - er - lov - in' light on me.

Worried Man

Traditional arranged by Brian Ley

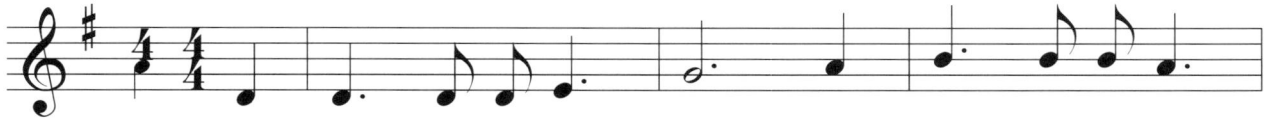

It takes a wor-ried man to sing a wor-ried

song, It takes a wor-ried man to sing a wor-ried

song, It takes a wor-ried man to sing a wor-ried

song, I'm wor-ried now, but I won't be wor-ried long._____

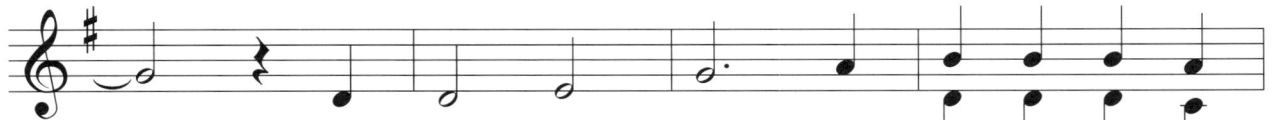

_____ The train I ride is six-teen coa-ches

long, The train I ride is six-teen coa-ches

long, The train I ride is six-teen coa-ches

long, But the one I love____ was on that train and gone.____

____ It takes a wor-ried man to sing a wor-ried

song, It takes a wor-ried man to sing a wor-ried

song, It takes a wor-ried man to sing a wor-ried

song, I'm wor-ried now, but I won't be wor-ried long,____

____ I'm wor-ried now, but I won't be wor-ried long.____

MUSICAL ELEMENTS

Pitch; Duration; Texture; Structure

SPECIFIC OBJECTIVES

■ Playing a blues scale melody and inventing words   ■ Playing an accompaniment   ■ Inventing a rhythm pattern

KEY WORDS

Blues, phrase, repeats, rests

RESOURCES

■ Percussion instruments with pitches D F A C' D'   ■ Non-pitched percussion

Making a Blues Song

ACTIVITIES	WATCHPOINTS

■ *Composing a Blues song*

Seat the class in a semicircle. Make the pitches D' C' A F D available on a pitched percussion instrument and place it in the middle of the semicircle. Play the following melody pattern fairly slowly to the class: D' C' A D A F D. Play it several times so that the class can sing the pitches to 'ooh'. Ask individuals to come and imitate your actions.

Ask the class to try singing the words 'Old man blues is on my trail' to the melody pattern. **W❶**

W❶ *Remind them that blues are sad songs about everyday living and that the expression 'feeling blue' means feeling sad.*

Then ask them to invent their own new words, for the same melody pattern, about feeling 'blue', e.g. rainy day, too much homework, video player broken, etc. Write up good ideas on the board. Explain that the melody should repeat once. Sing examples through with a repeat in each case.

Now ask individuals to come out and improvise a third melody line. It must start on A and finish on low D. The words of this line must follow on from the repeated first line and should end with a rhyme, e.g. 'Old man blues is on my trail, Old man blues is on my trail, Today is maths and I might fail.' Help all the class to sing the examples and choose some favourites to memorise. **W❷**

W❷ *Record or write down the songs for follow up work*

FOLLOW UP

Help the class to add rhythmic patterns to their blues songs. Practise a simple alternating knee brush and finger click at a steady tempo. When it is secure sing some of the songs invented in the previous session with the rhythmic accompaniment.

EXTENSION ACTIVITIES

Give further opportunities for individuals to make up their own blues using the same prescription. Encourage them to invent more than one verse.

SUPPORT ACTIVITIES

Ask children to practise the simple rhythmic pattern as in the Follow Up, and then transfer it on to non-pitched percussion.

ASSESSMENT POINTS

Make a note of those children who:
  • can compose a blues melody and words;   • can play a simple accompaniment;   • can invent a rhythmic accompanying pattern.

Assessment for Unit 3

Using some aspects of the checklist below you may identify what the children are able to do when they have followed Unit 3.

MUSICAL ACTIVITIES

PERFORMING:

- sing expressively;
- sing in tune;
- sing with good breath control;
- sing in style;
- sing confidently in three parts;
- perform a rhythm accompaniment;
- play a simple accompaniment;
- maintain a steady beat;
- perform a hand jive;
- find and play the melody of a song on instruments.

COMPOSING:

- improvise a rhythmic pattern over a steady beat;
- invent a rhythm accompaniment;
- compose a blues melody and words;
- compose, demonstrating understanding of style;
- invent and perform a hand jive;
- devise appropriate movements to a song.

LISTENING AND APPRAISING:

- listen with concentration;
- identify soprano and bass voices;
- identify different instrumental timbres;
- identify traditional and contemporary features;
- identify different musical styles;
- understand technical terms for dynamics;
- talk about the music they hear and compose using appropriate language;
- discuss music by Gershwin;
- talk about contrasting moods;
- respond imaginatively with language or art to the mood of the music.

About Unit 4
Rounds and descants

This unit explores different kinds of song structures, including rounds and descants, and through them gives the children opportunities to develop their ability to sing and to maintain an independent part. The unit also provides an insight into different historical contexts and forms, from 'Sumer is Icumen In' (a melody dating back to the 13th century), through the classical period with Mozart's *Magic Flute*, to the late 19th century and Gilbert and Sullivan operetta.

The concept of texture is reinforced, looking at how melodic lines interweave and complement each other, and so is the concept of timbre, giving children practice in identifying different vocal qualities.

Lessons
1 Dona Nobis Pacem
2 Sumer Is Icumen In
3 Are You Listening? Farandole
4 Good News
5 Operetta
6 Mozart's Magic Bells

TARGETS FOR UNIT 4

The following questions will help you identify what the children know, understand and can do. The particular focus will be on assessing their ability to listen and appraise what they hear, to identify texture and timbre, and the degree to which they have developed independent singing skills.

- Can the children identify the different singing voices?
- Can they perceive music in a number of different parts?
- How well do they sing an independent part?
- Can they use a round structure in their composing?

Dona Nobis Pacem

Traditional

MUSICAL ELEMENTS
Pitch; Dynamics; Texture; Structure

SPECIFIC OBJECTIVES
■ Singing a round in three parts ■ Singing with good vocal technique, pitch, dynamics and phrasing

KEY WORDS
Intonation, articulation, round

RESOURCES
■ CD 2 Tracks 11 and 12 'Dona Nobis Pacem' ■ Photocopy Sheet 33

Dona Nobis Pacem

ACTIVITIES

■ *Listening to the song* **W1**
Play Track 12 and ask the children to describe the structure of the song. *(It is a round, first sung in unison and then in parts.)* Play the recording again to see if the children can distinguish how many parts or 'lines' there are. *(Three.)* Ask them to notice also how the round stops. *(As it began, line by line, leaving a single line at the end.)*

■ *Singing the song*
Spend some time learning how to pronounce the words, using the model on the recording. **W2**
Using Track 12 with the balance control turned to the left, play the song through several times to familiarise the children with the melody. Ask them to join in when they can. Encourage them to sing quietly and to make their breath last for a whole line. **W3**
When they are singing the whole song confidently, turn the balance control to the right and ask them to sing with the accompaniment. The other parts will come in on the recording.

WATCHPOINTS

W1 *Track 11 has the voices on the left and the instruments on the right. Track 12 has the voice parts split between left and right.*

W2 *The Latin words 'dona nobis pacem' mean 'give us peace'.*
W3 *It is important to aim for a smooth and flowing line, good intonation or tuning, and clear diction (articulation). Singing quietly will help breathing and also allow them to hear the part singing on the recording.*

FOLLOW UP
When the whole melody has been learnt thoroughly and can be sung through, choose six of the most confident singers. Ask them to pair up and be the leaders of three groups. Explain that these singers will be asked to experiment to see if they can sing in three parts as on the recording. As they start to sing, choose other children to go and join each of the groups and join in until all the class is standing in a circle singing to each other.

EXTENSION ACTIVITIES
Encourage groups of three children to practise singing the round together as a trio. Challenge them to sing several repeats and then to end the round all together on the last pitch of each line (F), which can then fade out.

SUPPORT ACTIVITIES
If necessary, take the less confident singers to one side, while the others engage in the extension activity, and go through the melody again.

ASSESSMENT POINTS
Make a note of those children who:
  • can maintain an individual part in a round;   • sing with good articulation, intonation and breath control.

Sumer is I-cumen In

John of Fornsete

Sum - er is i - cum - en in,——— loud - e sing cuck - oo!

Grow - eth weed and blow - eth mead and springs the wood a - new.

Sing cuck - oo! Ewe now blea - teth af - ter lamb, loud

af - ter calf the cow. Bul - lock star - teth, buck re - ver - teth,

mer - ry sing cuck - oo! Cuck - oo, cuck - oo,———

well sing - eth thou cuck - oo, Nor cease thee nev - er now!

MUSICAL ELEMENTS
Pitch; Duration; Texture; Structure

SPECIFIC OBJECTIVES
- Learning about texture ■ Singing a round in several parts
- Performing pitched and rhythmic accompaniments

KEY WORDS
Drone, ostinato, round, in canon, unison

RESOURCES
■ CD 2 Tracks 13 and 14 'Sumer is Icumen In' ■ Pitched and non-pitched percussion instruments ■ Any other instruments played by the children ■ Photocopy Sheets 34, 35 and 36

Sumer Is Icumen In

ACTIVITIES

■ Learning about the song
Explain that 'Sumer is Icumen In' was written down in the 13th century in Reading, Berkshire, and is one of the earliest pieces of music written to be sung in parts. Play Track 13 several times, focusing the children's listening each time. Ask: How many vocal parts are there? *(Two.)* How do the voices enter? *(First in unison, then in turn, in a round.)* Remind them that a technical word for 'singing in a round' is 'in canon', and help them to hear the accompaniment ostinato which is also played in canon, and the bass drone. **W1**

■ Singing the song
When the children are familiar with the tune, let them join in with Track 14, singing to 'la'. Turn the balance control to the left to focus on the melody. Give out Photocopy sheet 34. Go over the words carefully and explain the old spellings. Practise saying and chanting the words to the rhythm of the song to obtain clear diction. **W2**

When the class can sing the words with Track 14, turn the balance control to the right to bring in the second vocal part. Then divide the class into two groups and sing the song as a round. Use Track 13 with the balance control turned to the right for the accompaniment only.

WATCHPOINTS

W1 *Using Track 13, turn the balance control to the right to focus on the accompaniment.*

W2 *The words mean: 'Summer is coming in. Loudly sing "cuckoo". The weeds/wild flowers grow, and new growth in the woods springs to life. The ewe bleats after the lamb and the calf calls loudly to the cow. The bullock jumps up, the buck (male deer) goes to eat the new grass. Merrily sing "cuckoo". Sing "cuckoo" well and never stop.'*

FOLLOW UP
Give out Photocopy sheet 35. With the whole class, practise the four ostinato patterns, using body sounds (clapping, clicking, etc.) or non-pitched percussion. Chant the word patterns to help rhythmic accuracy. Let the children decide the order, instrumentation and combination of parts to accompany their singing, and practise putting them together. Try different combinations and discuss the different textures created.

EXTENSION ACTIVITIES
Ask the children who learn instruments to use Photocopy sheet 36 to learn the ostinato or the drone to play as an accompaniment. Have them play with the class rhythmic accompaniment. Recorder players might add the melody line. This round will actually fit up to six parts. See how many parts the more confident children can maintain by singing and playing.

SUPPORT ACTIVITIES
Give less able children further practice in arranging and performing rhythm ostinato patterns.

ASSESSMENT POINTS
Make a note of those children who:
- can maintain an individual part in a round; • perform a rhythmic accompaniment accurately as part of an ensemble; • can perform an ostinato part; • can play a drone steadily and in time; • understand texture;
- demonstrate an understanding of the historical background.

Sumer is Icumen In
accompaniments

1   

    Sing   cuck   -   oo

2   

    Loud - ly   sing   cuck - oo

3   

    Sum - er   is   i - cum - en   in

4   

    Now   now

Sumer Is Icumen In

Drone

violin, recorder
pitched percussion

clarinet

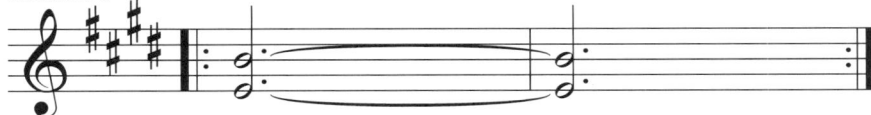

cello

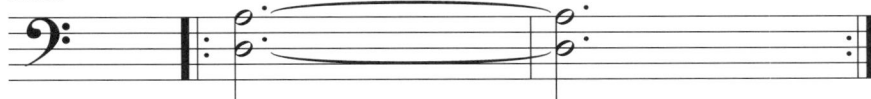

Ostinato

violin, recorder
pitched percussion

clarinet

cello

Farandole from L'Arlésienne

Georges Bizet

	structure	timbre	texture	dynamics	tempo
1	A	whole orchestra	hymn-like	forte (loud)	moderato (moderately fast)
2	A	violins and lower strings	in canon	mezzo forte (fairly loud)	allegro (fast)
3	B	woodwind melody with strings	melody with accompaniment	piano (quiet) crescendo (getting louder)	allegro (fast)
4	B	whole orchestra	melody with accompaniment	mezzo forte (fairly loud)	allegro (fast)
5	A	whole orchestra	unison	forte (loud)	allegro (fast)
6	B	woodwind melody with strings	melody with accompaniment	piano (quiet)	allegro (fast)
7	A	whole orchestra	unison	mezzo forte (fairly loud)	allegro (fast)
8	B	woodwind melody with strings, whole orchestra joins in	melody with accompaniment	piano (quiet) crescendo (getting louder)	allegro (fast)
9	A and B	strings (B) and brass (A)	melodies weaving, with accompaniment	forte (loud)	accelerando (getting faster)
10	A and B	strings (B) and brass (A), percussion	melodies weaving, with accompaniment	fortissimo (very loud)	presto (very fast)

MUSICAL ELEMENTS

All the elements

SPECIFIC OBJECTIVES

- Listening to music in canon
- Experimenting with imitation
- Composing in canon

KEY WORDS

In canon, incidental music, imitate, unison

RESOURCES

- CD 2 Track 15 Bizet: 'Farandole' from *L'Arlésienne*
- Pitched percussion
- Any instruments played by the children
- Photocopy Sheet 37

Are you Listening?
Farandole

| ACTIVITIES | WATCHPOINTS |

■ *Listening to a canon*

Play Track 15, and initiate a class discussion about the music. Pause at each recorded number to discuss the preceding section. Draw attention to the two contrasting melodies, and encourage the children to contribute suggestions about timbre, dynamics, tempo, and texture. Use Photocopy sheet 37 as you think appropriate. **W❶**

■ *Learning about Bizet*

Help the children to understand a little about Georges Bizet (1838 – 1875). Explain that he was a French composer, particularly famous for the opera *Carmen*. This 'Farandole' is a traditional French folk melody which Bizet arranged as part of the incidental music for a play called *The Girl from Arles (L'arlesienne)*.

W❶ *Photocopy sheet 37 may be used in three ways: for teacher information; complete, for the children to follow as they listen; or with any or all of the columns masked, for the children to complete.*

FOLLOW UP

Play a game of echo clapping with the class. Choose metre-in-three or metre-in-four and clap a series of short rhythm patterns which the class should imitate back each time. When they (and you) are competent, challenge them to listen for each new pattern, while they are still clapping the previous one (clapping in canon with you).

EXTENSION ACTIVITIES

Ask pairs of more able children to compose a short piece in canon using pitched percussion or their own instruments (pitches D, E F G A). They should experiment in imitating each other in canon, and try to sequence four patterns and perform them to the class. (A useful hint is to alternate patterns with long notes and patterns with short notes.)

SUPPORT ACTIVITIES

Give pairs of less confident children time to practise imitating clapping patterns, and trying them in canon with each other.

ASSESSMENT POINTS

Make a note of those children who:

- can imitate a given pattern;
- can imitate a pattern in canon;
- can compose a short piece in canon;
- recognise and understand the canon structure.

Good News

Traditional Spiritual

Swung

1 Good news, the char-iot's com-ing, Good news, the

2 Good news, the char-iot's com-ing, Good news, the

1 char-iot's com-ing, Good news, the char-iot's com-ing, And I

2 char-iot's com-ing, Good news, the char-iot's com-ing, And I

1 don't want her leave-a me be-hind. Good news, the

2 don't want her leave-a me be-hind. Good news, the

char - iot's com - ing,   Good news,   the   char - iot's com - ing,

char - iot's com - ing, Good   news,   the   char - iot's com - ing, Good

Good   news,   the   char - iot's com - ing, And I don't want her leave - a   me,

news,   the   char - iot's com - ing, And I don't want her   leave - a   me,

Don't want   her   leave - a   me,   Don't want   her   leave - a   me   be - hind.

Don't want   her   leave - a   me,   Don't want   her   leave - a   me   be - hind.

Good News

MUSICAL ELEMENTS
All the elements

SPECIFIC OBJECTIVES
- Singing a gospel song in two parts
- Clapping the off beat
- Adding a rhythmic accompaniment
- Improvising a rhythmic accompaniment

KEY WORDS
Off beat, gospel, solo, duet, coda

RESOURCES
- CD 2 Tracks 16 and 17 'Good News'
- Photocopy Sheets 38 and 39
- Non-pitched percussion instruments

ACTIVITIES	WATCHPOINTS

■ Listening to the song

Play Track 17 several times and focus the children's listening with questions. Ask: Who is singing? *(Two women.)* How are the words split between the voices? *('Good News' is sung by one voice and imitated by the other.)* Is the song a solo or a duet? *(A duet—two parts.)* Is the music calm or lively? *(Lively.)* What happens at the end? *(The singers improvise a coda.)* Explain that it is typical of a style called gospel in which the song usually tells a biblical or religious story. **W1**

W1 *Gospel songs are often known as spirituals.*

■ Clapping the 'off beat'

Practise 'off beat' clapping with the class. Set up a steady beat in metre-in-four, and ask the children to slap their thighs on counts 1 and 3, and to clap on counts 2 and 4:

1	2	3	4	1	2	3	4
slap	clap	slap	clap	slap	clap	slap	clap

Gradually eliminate the thigh slap, leaving off-beat clapping.

Play Track 17 and help the children to clap the off beats with the recording. **W2**

W2 *The off beats are marked X on Photocopy sheet 38 and played on the tambourine on the recording.*

FOLLOW UP
When the children are familiar with the song use Track 17 with the balance control to help them learn each part in turn. Divide the class into two groups to sing the upper and lower part with the recording. Then use Track 16 with the balance control turned to the right and perform the song with the accompaniment. Encourage singing in gospel style, which is energetic and rhythmic, and finally add off-beat clapping.

EXTENSION ACTIVITIES
Ask more able children to find word patterns to use as ostinati and to clap or play these on non-pitched percussion. Have them 'layer' them on top of each other and play them to accompany the instrumental interlude between the verses.

SUPPORT ACTIVITIES
Encourage less confident singers to sing the melody line each time (verse 1 - upper line, verse 2 - lower line).

ASSESSMENT POINTS
Make a note of those children who:
- can sing in gospel style;
- can maintain a part independently;
- can clap the off beat;
- can improvise a rhythm accompaniment.

MUSICAL ELEMENTS

Pitch; Timbre; Texture; Structure

SPECIFIC OBJECTIVES

■ Understanding the concept of opera, operetta and musical
■ Listening to and identifying vocal timbres and textures
■ Discussing and writing about Gilbert and Sullivan

KEY WORDS

Opera, operetta, musical, solo, trio, quartet, chorus, soprano, contralto, tenor, bass

RESOURCES

■ CD 1 Track 18 'Are You Listening? Gilbert & Sullivan'; Track 19 Gilbert & Sullivan: 'The Policeman's Song' from *The Pirates of Penzance*
■ Photocopy Sheet 40   ■ Poster 4

Operetta

ACTIVITIES

■ *Learning about opera and operetta*

Revise the words for the four main voices: soprano, contralto, tenor, bass. Remind the children that a chorus is made up from many voices. Explain that a musical story which is acted out on stage can be an opera, an operetta or a musical. **W1**

■ *Listening to Gilbert and Sullivan* **W2**

Tell the children they are going to listen to five extracts from Gilbert and Sullivan operettas and decide how many voices are singing (texture) and what kind they are (timbre). Play Track 18 and ask the pupils to circle the appropriate descriptions on Photocopy sheet 40. Encourage the children to discuss the music, focusing on texture, timbre and mood, and the words of the song.

1. 'A Paradox' from *The Pirates of Penzance* (trio: contralto, tenor, bass)
2. 'A More Humane Mikado' from *The Mikado* (solo bass)
3. 'When the Foeman Bears His Steel' from *The Pirates of Penzance* (solo bass with men's chorus)
4. 'Brightly Dawns Our Wedding Day' from *The Mikado* (quartet: soprano, contralto, tenor, bass)
5. 'There Is Beauty in the Bellow of the Blast' from *The Mikado* (duet: contralto and tenor)

WATCHPOINTS

W1 *They all consist of songs which help to tell a story and are accompanied by an orchestra. The style of the music is the main difference between them. In many operas everything is sung, even when the characters 'speak' to each other or when they explain what is happening.*
An operetta is similar to an opera but it is often shorter, more light-hearted and includes spoken dialogue. A musical is similar to an operetta but is more 'popular' in style, and the singers usually use microphones.
W2 *Sir Arthur Sullivan (1842–1900) wrote the music for 14 operettas; the words were written by Sir William Gilbert (1836–1911).*

FOLLOW UP

Listen to Track 19. Ask the class which of the other five extracts it resembles, and why. Play Track 18 again. *(It is like extract 3.)* Help them to notice that both songs are for bass solo with men's chorus. Both use many repeated melodic and rhythmic phrases. 'When the Foeman Bears His Steel' is a call and response song, with the chorus singing the 'tarantara' response. 'The Policeman's Song' has several verses and the chorus echoes the soloist at the end of each line. The tempo slows right down (pauses) at the end of each verse.

EXTENSION ACTIVITIES

Ask the good writers to write about their favourite Gilbert and Sullivan song. Prompt them to write about the texture and timbre, and why they like it. Encourage them to research Gilbert & Sullivan in the library.

SUPPORT ACTIVITIES

Give the less confident writers more time to discuss the extracts with you, referring to Poster 4.

ASSESSMENT POINTS

Make a note of those children who:
• recognise different vocal timbres and textures;   • use terms like 'trio' and 'quartet' accurately.

Name _____

Date _____

Are you listening?
Gilbert & Sullivan

Circle all the appropriate words for each song.

1	A Paradox from *The Pirates of Penzance*	solo duet trio quartet chorus	men's chorus women's chorus mixed chorus	soprano contralto tenor bass
2	A More Humane Mikado from *The Mikado*	solo duet trio quartet chorus	men's chorus women's chorus mixed chorus	soprano contralto tenor bass
3	When the Foeman Bears His Steel from *The Pirates of Penzance*	solo duet trio quartet chorus	men's chorus women's chorus mixed chorus	soprano contralto tenor bass
4	Brightly Dawns Our Wedding Day from *The Mikado*	solo duet trio quartet chorus	men's chorus women's chorus mixed chorus	soprano contralto tenor bass
5	There Is Beauty in the Bellow of the Blast from *The Mikado*	solo duet trio quartet chorus	men's chorus women's chorus mixed chorus	soprano contralto tenor bass

Magic Bells
from The Magic Flute

Words translated from Schickaneder
Music by Wolfgang Amadeus Mozart

1. Oh___ lis - ten to mus - ic that is
2. It___ hangs in the star - light and de -

charm - ing our ears. La la la la la
scends to the ground. La la la la la

la la la la la la la la. This___
la la la la la la la la. I___

Sounds of MUSIC

Bells

mu - sic - al ma - gic from no - where ap -
ne - ver did hear such a ma - gi - cal

pears.
sound.

La la la la la la la la la
La la la la la la la la la

1.

2.

la la la la. This___ la.
la la la la. I___ la.

MUSICAL ELEMENTS

Timbre; Texture; Structure

SPECIFIC OBJECTIVES

■ Learning about Mozart's *The Magic Flute* ■ Listening to a trio
■ Singing a duet ■ Playing an accompaniment

KEY WORDS

Mozart, opera, trio, duet

RESOURCES

■ CD 2 Track 20 Mozart: *The Magic Flute* (excerpt); Tracks 21 and 22
'Magic Bells' ■ Photocopy Sheets 41 and 42 ■ Glockenspiel or
metallohone (or other metal pitched percussion)

Mozart's Magic Bells

ACTIVITIES	WATCHPOINTS

■ *Talking about* **The Magic Flute**

Explain that *The Magic Flute* (1791) is the last of Mozart's operas and
one of the most popular. **W❶**

One character is a bird-catcher, Papageno, who is given a set of magic
bells which help him to get out of trouble. He is about to be captured
when he plays the bells, and the gang who were to capture him sing
and dance happily instead.

W❶ *Wolfgang Amadeus Mozart lived at the end of the 18th century in Austria and his music is thought by some to be some of the most perfect music so far composed in Western Europe.*

■ *Listening to some music from* **The Magic Flute**

Explain that this is the music sung by the gang who tried to capture
Papageno and ended up under the spell of the magic bells. Play Track
20, which is sung in the original German. Ask: Is this a duet, a trio, or
a quartet? *(A trio.)*

■ *Singing the song*

Give out Photocopy sheets 41 and 42 and look through the words to
find out the meaning of the German words on Track 20. Play Track 22
for comparison. **W❷**

Turn the balance control to the left to isolate the upper melody and
help the children to learn to sing it. When they are confident turn
the balance control back and help them to perform the upper melody
against the lower line. Teach the lower line in the same way. **W❸**

W❷ *This is an easier duet version of the original trio.*

W❸ *The parts run in parallel just three pitches apart almost throughout. Singing in 'thirds' is a natural introduction to singing in parts.*

FOLLOW UP

Practise both parts with the recording. Divide the class into two groups, assign the upper and lower parts accordingly,
and sing in two parts together with Track 21. (Turn the balance control to the right to remove the recorded
singing.) Ask the two groups to swap parts next time.

EXTENSION ACTIVITIES

Help the keen and confident musicians to learn to play the bell part on Photocopy sheets 41 and 42. It can be played
on pitched percussion or on an electric keyboard with a suitable bell sound selected. Recorder or other wind players
may also be able to play this part. If they can, ask them to play while the class sing.

SUPPORT ACTIVITIES

Ask the less confident singers to sing the lower melody line and give them extra practice.

ASSESSMENT POINTS

Make a note of those children who:
- demonstrate a little knowledge of Mozart and *The Magic Flute*; • can sing a part in a duet; • can play a simple
melodic accompaniment; • select an appropriate accompaniment on a keyboard.

Assessment for Unit 4

Using some aspects of the checklist below, you may identify what the children are able to do when they have followed Unit 4.

MUSICAL ACTIVITIES

PERFORMING:

- sing in a gospel style;
- sing with good articulation, intonation and breath control;
- sing a part in a duet;
- maintain a part independently;
- maintain an individual part in a round;
- perform a rhythmic accompaniment accurately as part of an ensemble;
- play a simple melodic accompaniment;
- perform an ostinato part;
- play a drone steadily and in time;
- imitate a given pattern;
- imitate a pattern in canon;
- clap on the off beat.

COMPOSING:

- select an appropriate accompaniment on a keyboard;
- improvise a rhythm accompaniment;
- compose a short piece in canon.

LISTENING AND APPRAISING:

- demonstrate an understanding of texture;
- recognise and understand a canon structure;
- demonstrate an understanding of historical background;
- demonstrate a little knowledge of Mozart and The Magic Flute;
- recognise different vocal timbres (soprano, contralto, tenor, bass);
- identify the number of voices singing;
- use terms like trio and quartet accurately.

About Unit 5
Swinging

This unit focuses on duration, and looks forward to Key Stage 3 (S1 in Scotland) with its exploration of jazzy rhythms, on and off beats and syncopation. The songs and music are lively, with catchy rhythms and in all the lessons there is an emphasis on using clapping, clicking or playing percussion to recognise, identify and perform the rhythms of the music.

There is also an opportunity to learn about music of different styles from different times, countries and cultures, and to recognise and understand that rhythm is an essential part of all of them.

Lessons
1 Syncopation
2 African Chant
3 Song for Oxum
4 Are You Listening? Syncopation
5 Music's Mine
6 Improvising

TARGETS FOR UNIT 5

The following questions will help you to identify what the children know, understand and can do. You may also wish to check the assessment pages from other units if you are writing an end of year report.

- Do the children show a well developed sense of rhythm?
- Can they distinguish between on and off beats?
- Are they confident when playing percussion?
- Do they use the concepts they have learned in their compositions?

Syncopation

George Odam

A

Syn - co - pa - ted rhy - thm gets__ us dan - cing;

hands__ and feet are tap-ping, it's__ en - tran - cing. Fas - cin - a - tion

'cross__ the na - tion. Ev - ry - one loves syn - co - pa - tion.__

B

Can you hear those dan - cing feet tap - ping

C

to the beat with syn - co - pa - tion?__ Syn-co - pa-tion,

syn - co - pa-tion, ev'- ry-one dan - cing to the beat. Syn-co-pa - tion!

MUSICAL ELEMENTS
Duration; Structure

SPECIFIC OBJECTIVES
■ Singing expressively 'with a swing'

KEY WORDS
Swing, strong/on beat and weak/off beat

RESOURCES
■ CD 3 Track 1 'In the Mood'; Tracks 2 and 3 'Syncopation'　■ Poster 5
■ Photocopy Sheet 43　■ Non-pitched percussion instruments

Syncopation

ACTIVITIES

■ *Responding to swing music*

Discuss Poster 5 with the class. Ask: What shapes can you see? How would you describe the colours? Which pattern of shape and colour do you like best? Why? Do you think 'Swinging' is a good title for this picture? Why? Help the children to perceive the strong feeling of movement given by this arrangement of shapes and colours. **W1**

Lead the children to understand the musical meaning of the term 'swing music' *(music with a strong and compulsive beat)*. **W2**

To demonstrate swing style, play the recording of 'In the Mood'. Encourage the children to click their fingers with the beat and note whether they all choose the 'tick' (or strong/on beat), or the 'tock' (or weak/off beat). Talk about weak beats and strong beats, using the clock analogy. **W3**

Ask the class to practise saying 'tick, tock' repeatedly, whilst clicking their fingers on 'tick'. Then ask them to click on 'tock' waving their hands outwards on 'tick'.

■ *Learning the song*

Play Track 2 and ask the children to show the compulsive 'on' beat (tick) as they listen. Let them listen again and this time click on the off (tock) beat. Help them to identify the sound of the tap-dancing feet in the accompaniment. When they have heard the song enough, ask them to sing section A. You may wish to give out Photocopy sheet 43. **W4**

WATCHPOINTS

W1 *Vasily Kandinsky (Russian, 1866–1944) was one of the first abstract painters. He painted 'Swinging' in 1925. He said that when he listened to music he saw colours.*

W2 *The musical term 'swing' was first used for the music of the 1930s and 1940s big bands, led by musicians like Benny Goodman and Glenn Miller.*

W3 *We use the words 'tick, tock' rather than the more accurate 'tick, tick', because it is natural for our brains to divide beats into unequal pairs, one felt as a strong/on beat (tick) and the other as a weak/off beat (tock).*

W4 *The term 'syncopation' means placing a strong emphasis on the weak or off beat, thus upsetting the 'tick tock' pattern we naturally establish. This gives the music an element of surprise all the time and gives it a bright jumpy feeling which we often call 'jazzy'.*

FOLLOW UP
Revise the song, singing with Track 3. Ask: What happens at the end? *(Sections A and B are sung simultaneously. Use the balance control to highlight the separate parts.)* When they can sing both sections A and B confidently, divide the class into two groups. One group sings section A and the other sings section B at the same time. Swap parts. Working in pairs, ask the children to invent a hand jive that they can perform as they sing.

EXTENSION ACTIVITIES
Encourage more able musicians to develop a syncopated rhythm pattern to accompany this song. Ask any experienced (tap) dancers to invent a routine.

SUPPORT ACTIVITIES
Less confident children should be encouraged to play a non-pitched instrument on whichever of the strong or weak beats they can most clearly feel and manage.

ASSESSMENT POINTS
Make a note of those children who:
• sing expressively and rhythmically;　• can maintain an independent part;　• can invent a hand jive;　• can clap or click on and off the beat;　• understand off and on beat;　• can invent a syncopated accompaniment.

African Chant

Traditional

① Call

Wom ma mez une co - ma pas bon

Response

di a - pu - la, des na - né - na

② Call

nez à ba di a - pu - la

Response

di a - pu - la, des na - né - na

③ Call

Wow

Response

di a - pu - la, des na - né na.

MUSICAL ELEMENTS
Duration

SPECIFIC OBJECTIVES
■ Establishing the feel of on and off beats   ■ Performing a call part

KEY WORDS
Strong beat, weak beat, accent, jazzy

RESOURCES
■ CD 3 Tracks 4 and 5 'African Chant'   ■ Photocopy Sheet 44
■ Drum

African Chant

ACTIVITIES

■ *Performing the off beat*

Remind the class of the 'tick tock' rhythm encountered in Unit 5 Lesson 1. Discuss strong/on and weak/off beats. Strong accents on weak or off beats produce a lively, jazzy feel. Set up a steady beat on a drum and ask the children to pat the on beats on their knees. Then ask them to click their fingers on the off beats as well. Now remove the on beat pats and only click the off beats. Practice changing from on and off beats, on beats only and off beats only, using an agreed signal from you to show when to change.

■ *Singing the song*

Play Track 5, explaining that this is a call and response song and the class are to join in with the response as soon as they can. The words are: 'Di apula des nanéna'. **W❶**

■ *Singing, clapping and stamping*

As soon as the children are confident singing the response, encourage them to clap on the beat throughout. (Wom ma mez une co-ma pas bon, etc.) If they can manage this well help them to add a stamping rhythm. It has a 'ba-boom 2 3 4' pattern, and fits just before and on the first beat of the song, repeating every four clapped beats. **W❷**

WATCHPOINTS

W❶ *The words are a mixture of a West African language and French. It is a nonsense song.*

W❷ *The clapping and the stamping rhythm pattern are featured on the recording.*

FOLLOW UP
Ask the class to concentrate this time on the calls. There are three patterns. Ask: Which pattern is syncopated? *(The third one. It starts with a silent beat, making a heavy accent on the off beat 'Wow')* Help the class to learn the words and melody of the calls. (You may wish to hand out Photocopy sheet 44.) When they know both calls and response, divide the class into two groups and without the recording let them set up the clapped and stamped beats. One group sings the call, the other the response.

EXTENSION ACTIVITIES
Choose individuals who have learnt the song well to perform the call either on their own or as a group.

SUPPORT ACTIVITIES
Encourage those less able children who are able to clap the beat by asking them to play it on a drum or other suitable instrument.

ASSESSMENT POINTS
Make a note of those children who:
  • can play and move to on and off beats;   • can perform the call part in a call and response song.

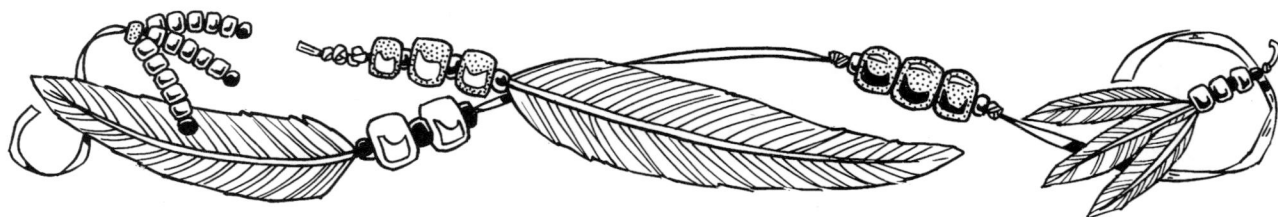

Song for Oxum

Traditional song from Brazil

Ye i ye___ o e o shoor a door,___

Ye i ye___ o e o shoor a door,___ Shoor i

shoor i fe - i - fe___ shoor a door,___ Shoor i

shoor i fe - i - fe___ shoor a door.___

MUSICAL ELEMENTS
Pitch; Duration; Timbre

SPECIFIC OBJECTIVES
■ Performing rhythm patterns accurately as an accompaniment
■ Recognising different percussion timbres ■ Listening to Brazilian music

KEY WORDS
Carnival, Oxum (pron: Oh-shoom), syncopated, ostinato

RESOURCES
■ CD 3 Track 6 'Song for Oxum' ■ Non-pitched percussion instruments
■ Photocopy Sheets 45 and 46

Song for Oxum

ACTIVITIES

■ *Listening and performing* **W1**

Play the introduction to Track 6 and press the pause button as the flute enters. Discuss with the class what part of the world they think this music might come from. **W2**

Listen to the first rhythm pattern on the conga drum again, and help the children to imitate it using their hands on the floor, desks etc. (short/long-short-short/long-short-short).

Help them to hear that the drum has two pitches—high and low—and decide which beats are which (low/high-high-low/high-high-low).

Remind them that a repeated pattern is called an ostinato.

The maracas come next. Ask the children to wiggle their fingers on the shaken long beat, and tap the two short beats in their palms. (Shake-tap-tap). Layer the conga and maracas lines together.

The third ostinato is syncopated and is the most complex. As they learn to tap this pattern help the children to hear that it is twice as long as the others and is played on the agogo or two-tone cowbells. It may be useful to use the word pattern 'Listen <u>to</u> the carnival, high, high, low, low'.

The last pattern has the same rhythm as the first two. Encourage the children to tap each of the patterns separately and then, with the help of the recording, layer them in one on top of the other.

WATCHPOINTS

W1 *The accompaniment consists of four percussion ostinato patterns, which come in one after the other. Patterns 1, 2 and 4 have the same rhythm. They are shown on Photocopy sheet 46.*

W2 *It comes from Brazil and is performed during the carnivals held there every February. The song is for a beautiful African goddess of the waters, still worshipped by the descendants of the Nigerian slaves who were taken to Brazil hundreds of years ago. The words were taken down phonetically from a Brazilian folk singer. The language is unknown.*

FOLLOW UP
The song encourages us to sway like the waves as we sing. As soon as they can, let the children sway as they sing, adding a percussion accompaniment (see Extension Activities).

EXTENSION ACTIVITIES
Ask the more confident performers to play the rhythm patterns on percussion instruments they have chosen to imitate the sounds on the recording. They might use the notation on Photocopy sheet 46.

SUPPORT ACTIVITIES
Provide the largest drum for a less well co-ordinated child to provide a steady beat to lead a swaying procession round the classroom.

ASSESSMENT POINTS
Make a note of those children who:
• perform rhythm patterns accurately; • can play a percussion accompaniment; • recognise different percussion sounds; • select appropriate instruments.

Song for Oxum accompaniment

1. conga

1	2	3	4	1	2	3	4
(low) high		high	low	high		high	low

2. maracas

1	2	3	4	1	2	3	4
shake		tap	tap	shake		tap	tap

3. agogo

1	2	3	4	1	2	3	4
lis - ten to the car - ni - val,				high	high	low	low

4. drum

1	2	3	4	1	2	3	4
long		short	short	long		short	short

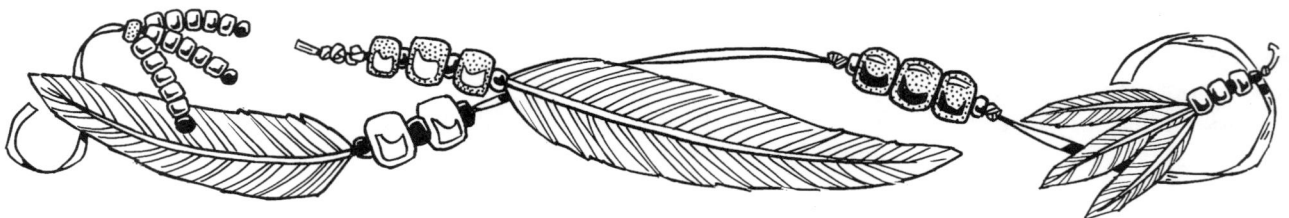

MUSICAL ELEMENTS
Duration

SPECIFIC OBJECTIVES
■ Making links with visual art and syncopation   ■ Identifying music with strong syncopation;   ■ Comparing music of different styles

KEY WORDS
Jazzy, syncopated

RESOURCES
■ CD 3 Track 7 'Are You Listening? Syncopation'   ■ Photocopy Sheet 47
■ Poster 5

Are You Listening?
Syncopation

ACTIVITIES

WATCHPOINTS

■ *Listening and appraising*

Display Poster 5. Ask the children to choose some words from these pairs which will best describe this painting, giving reasons for their choice: cold/warm, rhythmic/non-rhythmic, lively/calm, syncopated/not syncopated, jazzy/classical. *(A list might read 'warm, rhythmic, lively, syncopated, jazzy', but there is no hard and fast answer.)*

Remind the class that syncopation livens up music by accentuating the unexpected.

Give out Photocopy sheet 47 and explain that they will hear six short extracts of music, some of which will be syncopated and some which will not. Play Track 7 at least twice, reminding the children not to write anything the first time, but to wait for the second playing before they respond by circling the appropriate words.

Let them work privately and take in the papers before you go over the examples again, pausing after each one to discuss it. Encourage the children to make comparisons between the pieces. **W❶**

The extracts are:
1. Handel: *The Arrival of the Queen of Sheba* (not syncopated) (18th century orchestral)
2. Walton: *Portsmouth Point* (syncopated) (20th century orchestral)
3. Neff/Lewis/Moross: *The Big Country* (syncopated) (20th century film music)
4. Beethoven: *Für Elise* (not syncopated) (19th century piano)
5. Gray/De-Lange: *String of Pearls* (syncopated) (20th century swing)
6. Mozart: *A Musical Joke,* Rondo (not syncopated) (18th century orchestral)

W❶ *Listening to the extracts and discussing them is the most important part of the lesson. The results should show you something of the effectiveness of what you have taught, and possibly give some guidance to individual musical ability.*

FOLLOW UP
Make opportunities for children to listen to the extracts during the week. Encourage them to discuss, write or draw how the music makes them feel.

ASSESSMENT POINTS
Make a note of those children who:
• can identify syncopated music;   • discuss music they hear, using appropriate musical terminology;   • compare music of different styles;   • respond imaginatively to music they hear.

Name _____

Date _____

Are you listening?
Syncopation

Some of these pieces are highly syncopated. Some are not.
Decide which is which.
Tick one box for each piece.

		Syncopated	Not Syncopated
1	Handel: The Arrival of the Queen of Sheba	☐	☐
2	Walton: Portsmouth Point	☐	☐
3	Neff/Lewis/Moross: The Big Country	☐	☐
4	Beethoven: Für Elise	☐	☐
5	Gray/De-Lange: String of Pearls	☐	☐
6	Mozart: A Musical Joke	☐	☐

Music's Mine

George Odam

Music, music, music sur- rounds us.

Mu - sic mu - sic sur -

har - mon - y, mel - o - dy and rhy - thm com - bine.

rounds us al - ways.

Mu - sic, music, mu - sic a - round us when we

Mu - sic a - round us when we

play or we sing we're feel - ing fine.

sing we all feel fine.

Har - mon - y mel - o - dy rhy - thm text - ture and

Har - mon - y mel - o - dy rhy - thm

struc - ture mak - ing Mu - sic, mu - sic, mu - sic a - bound - ing

tex - ture, struc - ture. Mu - sic a - bound - ing

all the day long____ sing - ing a song____

all the day long____ sing - ing a song____

sing - ing it strong - ly for mu - sic's mine!

sing - ing it strong - ly for mu - sic's mine!

MUSICAL ELEMENTS

All the elements

SPECIFIC OBJECTIVES

■ Learning to sing a song in two parts ■ Talking about musical elements

KEY WORDS

Harmony, melody, rhythm, texture, structure

RESOURCES

■ CD 3 Tracks 8 and 9 'Music's Mine' ■ Photocopy Sheets 48 and 49

Music's Mine

ACTIVITIES	WATCHPOINTS

■ *Listening and appraising*

Play Track 9 and ask the children to tell you what the song is about. What are the key words? *(Harmony, melody, rhythm, texture, structure.)* Go over these elements of music and revise with the class what each of them means and where they have experienced them in other lessons. Ask: What was special about the texture of the voice parts in the repeat? *(There are two vocal lines.)* **W1**

■ *Singing the song*

Focus attention on the upper line and use the balance control to help the children to learn it. Stress the need for plenty of breath and for good posture. Above all, encourage singing with a smile. When they are confident let them sing the top line with the recording, as well as they can. **W2**

W1 *Use Track 9 with the balance control turned to the left to focus on the upper line, and turned to the right to focus on the lower line. Use Track 8 with the balance control turned to the right to remove all the recorded voices.*

W2 *You may wish to hand out Photocopy sheets 48 and 49.*

FOLLOW UP

Concentrate on the lower line in the repeated verse. Use the balance control to help the children to learn this line as a melody on its own. When they have grasped it let them sing it with the recording during the repeat verse of the song, having sung the upper line during the first verse. If they are confident, try dividing the class into two groups, one for each part, and see if they can manage to sing both at once. If this is successful, exchange parts and try again. When they become really confident, help them to sing in two parts without the voices on the CD.

EXTENSION ACTIVITIES

Encourage pairs of children to sing in two parts as a duet.

SUPPORT ACTIVITIES

It will be quite enough for the less able children to sing the upper part only.

ASSESSMENT POINTS

Make a note of those children who:
• demonstrate an understanding of musical elements; • sing with good posture; • sing an independent line confidently; • can sing in two parts.

Name _____

Date _____

Are you listening?
In the Mood

Did you hear any syncopation?_ _ _ _ _ _ _ _ _ _ _ _ _ _ _ _ _ _ _ _

Did the music have a strong swing?_ _ _ _ _ _ _ _ _ _ _ _ _ _ _ _ _ _

What timbres did you distinguish?_ _ _ _ _ _ _ _ _ _ _ _ _ _ _ _ _ _ _

_ _

_ _

_ _

_ _

What texture does this music have?_ _ _ _ _ _ _ _ _ _ _ _ _ _ _ _ _ _ _

_ _

_ _

_ _

What do you like about this music, and why? _ _ _ _ _ _ _ _ _ _ _ _ _ _

_ _

_ _

_ _

_ _

_ _

MUSICAL ELEMENTS

Pitch; Duration; Timbre; Texture

SPECIFIC OBJECTIVES

■ Listening and responding to lively and syncopated music
■ Composing a sound picture from a visual stimulus ■ Conducting a class improvisation/composition

KEY WORDS

Syncopation, graphic score

RESOURCES

■ CD 3 Track 1 'In the Mood' ■ Pitched and non-pitched instruments
■ Poster 5 ■ Pointer ■ Photocopy Sheet 50

Improvising

ACTIVITIES

■ *Composing a sound picture*

Display Poster 5 and ask the class to imagine that it is a graphic score. Decide which way up you wish to use it and how it will be 'read' (e.g. from left to right, top to bottom, etc.). **W❶**

The task is to improvise a piece of music called 'Swinging' involving the whole class. Here are some possibilities, but the result will be up to you and the class:

- Colours might equal timbre or dynamics
- 'Top' could mean high pitch and 'bottom' low
- Curved lines could mean swooping melodies
- Wavy lines could mean wavy melodies

Think also about the background of the picture and the spaces between the objects, and how this equates with silence or background sounds.

Control the improvisation yourself and, through discussion with the children, use whatever instruments are available. Tape record the result, and encourage the class to discuss, refine and improve their work.

WATCHPOINTS

W❶ *It will be helpful to use a pointer to show which part of the painting is being used.*

FOLLOW UP

Play Track 1, 'In the Mood'. (You may wish to use Photocopy sheet 50.) Stimulate class discussion with questions. Ask: Did you hear any syncopation? *(Yes.)* Did the music have a strong swing? *(Yes.)* What timbres did you distinguish? Orchestra? Rock band? Chorus? *(Instruments: swing band.)* What texture does this music have? Solo and accompaniment? Many instruments at once? One solo instrument? *(Many instruments.)* What do you like about this music and why? Give opportunities for children to paint their own 'swinging' picture, entitled 'In the Mood'.

EXTENSION ACTIVITIES

Challenge a small group of more able children to invent their own version of 'Swinging'.

SUPPORT ACTIVITIES

Allow less able children the chance to be the 'controller' or 'conductor' of the improvised piece.

ASSESSMENT POINTS

Make a note of those children who:
- make appropriate responses when appraising music;   • can improvise a sound piece from a visual stimulus;
- can conduct a class composition;   • respond to music through art.

Assessment for Unit 5

Using some aspects of the checklist below, you may identify what the children are able to do when they have followed Unit 5.

MUSICAL ACTIVITIES

PERFORMING:

- sing expressively and rhythmically;
- maintain an independent part;
- clap or click on and off the beat;
- play on and off beats;
- perform the call part in a call and response song;
- perform rhythm patterns accurately;
- play a percussion accompaniment;
- sing with good posture;
- sing an independent line confidently;
- sing in two parts;
- conduct a class composition.

COMPOSING:

- invent a hand jive;
- invent a syncopated accompaniment;
- select appropriate instruments;
- improvise a sound piece from a visual stimulus.

LISTENING AND APPRAISING:

- understand on and off beat;
- move to on and off beats;
- recognise different percussion sounds;
- identify syncopated music;
- discuss music they hear, using appropriate musical terminology;
- compare music of different styles;
- demonstrate an understanding of musical elements;
- make appropriate responses when appraising music;
- respond to music through art;
- respond imaginatively to music they hear.

About Unit 6
Since the 30s

The songs and music in this unit give us a picture of popular music since the 1930s, from the war-time 'White Cliffs of Dover' through the brass band tradition of the 1950s, the pop music of Cliff Richard in the 1960s, and the music of ABBA in the 1970s.

There is also further work on off beat rhythms, anticipating work in Key Stage 3 (S1 in Scotland). There are opportunities for revising work on sound pictures with the 'Night in the Blitz' and a final composing challenge is set in the last lesson—to compose an anthem. This could be a collaborative effort encouraging those who are more talented at writing to provide words and those learning instruments to provide the melody.

Lessons
1 We're Going to the Country
2 The White Cliffs of Dover
3 Composing 'Blitz Night'
4 Listen to the Band
5 Summer Holiday
6 Thank You for the Music
7 This Is Our Country

TARGETS FOR UNIT 6

The following questions will help you identify what the children know, understand and can do. You will need to use them in conjunction with other assessment questions from other units to help you record their achievements as they move on to Key Stage 3 (S1 in Scotland).

- How confidently and rhythmically do the children demonstrate their feel for the beat?
- How expressively do they sing and do they memorize accurately?
- How good are they at organising ideas, inventing and sequencing sounds, composing melodies?
- Are they able to record or notate their ideas effectively?
- How confidently do they talk about music?

Tenor trombone

Flugelhorn Bb bass Bb cornet Horn Bass trombone Eb cornet Baritone Euphonium Eb bass

Sounds of MUSIC
POSTER 6
YEAR 6/P7

We're Going to the Country
from Blitz!

Lionel Bart

We're go - ing to the coun - try,

Look af - ter your- self, Sid - dy, look af - ter your-

We're going to see the cows.

self

Look af - ter your- self, Tom-my, look af - ter your-

We're going to have a real bath

self

Eat three meals a day,

in a love - ly house

ev - 'ry day

Please don't cry while

Sounds of MUSIC

1: They call it 'va - cu - a - tion

2: you're a - way___ Look af - ter your-self, Tom - my, look af - ter your-

1: They take you to the sta - tion

2: self. Look af - ter your-self, Cath - y, look af - ter your-

1: They put you on a train Let's hope it does - n't

2: self. Bye - bye, Bye -

1: rain. We're go - ing to the coun - try

2: bye Bye - bye.

We're Going to the Country

MUSICAL ELEMENTS
Timbre; Texture; Structure

SPECIFIC OBJECTIVES
■ Learning to sing a dramatic song expressively ■ Recreating the 'operatic' scene dramatically ■ Talking about the structure and setting

KEY WORDS
Phrase, repeat

RESOURCES
■ CD 3 Tracks 10 and 11 'We're Going to the Country' ■ Photocopy Sheets 51 and 52

ACTIVITIES

WATCHPOINTS

■ *Listening and appraising*

Give out Photocopy sheets 51 and 52. Having explained the concept of children being evacuated during World War II, play Track 11 and ask the class to listen to the words for information about what it was like to live in a big City during the War. What did the city children (evacuees) think they would have in the country that they didn't have at home? *(A real bath.)* What animals did they expect to see? *(Cows.)* **W1**

Listen to Track 11 again, for repeated sections. Help the children to hear and see that the first three phrases are of similar shape, but each phrase is subtly different at the end. Phrase 5 is the same as phrase 1, and phrase 6 is similar to phrase 2, but the last two phrases are interestingly 'stitched' together and hurry the song to its conclusion. **W2**

Help the class to notice that the verse is repeated three times. Ask: What happens to the texture the third time? *(There is an added vocal part for the worried adults saying goodbye to their children)* **W3**

Discuss with the children what this new texture adds to the scene dramatically. If it had just been spoken would it have been more or less effective? Ask: Is there any suggestion of wartime feel in the music? *(The clear 1 2 3 4 marching beat.)*

W1 *Many poorer people had only a portable tin bath by the fireside. Usually one lot of bath water did for the whole family. This applied equally well in city or country. Many city children had never seen cows before they were evacuated.*

W2 *The phrases are marked on Photocopy sheets 51 and 52.*

W3 *Turn the balance control to the right to focus on the adult part.*

FOLLOW UP
When the children feel confident, encourage them to join in. When it comes to the third verse they should sing quietly and try to listen also to the voices of the worried Mums.

EXTENSION ACTIVITIES
With plenty of reference to the recording a few good singers may be able to tackle the part of the worried parents. If they can do this, let them help to prepare a class dramatic version of a station on evacuation day, to be performed to other children in assembly.

SUPPORT ACTIVITIES
Practise the song without the 'worried parents' singers, so that the main group sings confidently. Help them to imitate the Cockney accents of the children on the recording. A full throated style of singing may well encourage some children who are reluctant to sing to join in more willingly.

ASSESSMENT POINTS
Make a note of those children who:
- sing with expression; • maintain a second part confidently • can identify the structure of the song;
- comment well on texture and timbre.

MUSICAL ELEMENTS
Pitch; Structure

SPECIFIC OBJECTIVES
■ Singing with expression ■ Experiencing a sentimental song from World War II ■ Recognising how music can reflect time and place

KEY WORDS
Crooning, ballad, verse, refrain, lyrics

RESOURCES
■ CD 3 Track 12 'The White Cliffs of Dover'; Track 13 Coates: *The Dambusters March* ■ Poster 6 ■ Photocopy Sheets 53 and 54

The White Cliffs of Dover

ACTIVITIES

■ *Listening to and singing the song*

Give out Photocopy sheets 53 and 54, and explain that a ballad is a sentimental song, usually with a verse and refrain structure. The verse often sets the scene and explains the story, while the refrain gives the mood and feeling. Play Track 12, pausing at the end of the verse. Ask the class what the song is about. Help them to focus on the important lyrics. **W1**

Play the refrain and ask the children to express the mood it creates. *(Warm, looking forward, confident, sentimental.)* Explain that this was one of the most popular songs in Britain during World War II and was sung by Vera Lynn. Ask the children to hum along with the recording as they listen to the refrain. When they are confident encourage them to sing the lyrics of the refrain. Encourage them to sing gently and quietly, with lots of breath so as not to split up the long phrases. **W2**

WATCHPOINTS

W1 *'Braving those angry skies' refers to the pilots, 'thumbs up' still means the same now, but was particularly a sign from the pilot to the ground crew to pull away the blocks or 'chocks' from the fighter plane wheels just before take-off.*
W2 *This kind of gentle singing, amplified by a microphone, was popular in the 1940s and was called 'crooning'.*

FOLLOW UP
The spirit of Britain during the war can also be felt by listening to Track 13, music by Eric Coates used in the famous film 'The Dambusters' commemorating the RAF's exploits in 1943. Ask: What mood does the music convey? *(Confident, strong.)* What does this suggest about the people of Britain during the war? *(Confident and ready to fight.)*
Using Tracks 11, 12 and 13, encourage some of the more able children to make up a dramatic sequence by linking the songs with improvised movement and drama that will tell the story of life in Britain during World War II.

SUPPORT ACTIVITIES
Encourage reticent singers to join in with the song by humming rather than singing the words.

ASSESSMENT POINTS
Make a note of those children who:
  • sing with good breath control; • sing gently; • talk about the mood of the music; • understand how music can reflect time and place.

The White Cliffs of Dover

Words by Nat Burton
Music by Walter Kent

Verse

I'll nev-er for-get the peo-ple I met brav-ing those an-gry skies; I re-mem-ber well as the sha-dows fell, The light of hope in their eyes. And tho' I'm far a-way, I still can hear them say, 'Thumbs up!' For when the dawn comes up:

Refrain

There'll be Blue-birds ov - er the white cliffs of Do-ver, to -

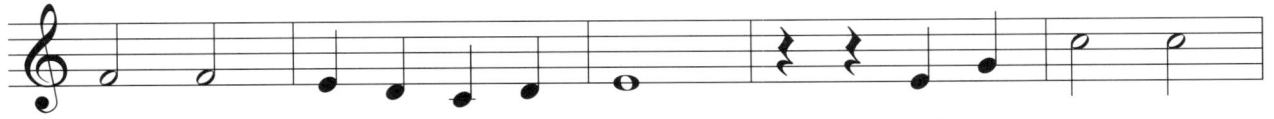

mor - row, just you wait and see There'll be love and

laugh - ter and peace ev - er af - ter, to - mor - row,

when the world is free._____ The shep-herd will tend his sheep, The

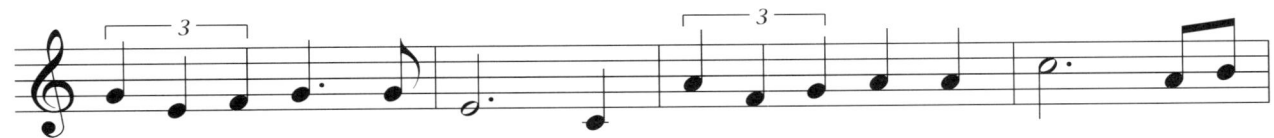

val - ley will bloom a - gain, And Jim-my will go to sleep in his

own lit - tle room a - gain. There'll be Blue - birds ov - er the

white cliffs of Do - ver, to - mor - row, just you wait and see.

A Night in the Blitz
Autumn 1940

We couldn't get to sleep that night, so we sat up in bed and peeped through the curtains. There were no street lights and it was very dark. We could see the searchlights moving across the sky, looking for planes.

Suddenly a terrifying wail moaned upwards into the night and seemed to hang there, shrieking at us. We heard Mum shout "It's an air raid! Quick! Into the shelter." As the siren died away we dashed downstairs with our gas masks and squeezed under the kitchen table with Mum and Gran. It was a special table, called a Morrison shelter, with a steel top and bottom and steel mesh sides. It was very hot and stuffy under there, but we felt safer. Everything went very quiet, although a few dull thuds and booms could be heard in the distance – the guns at the coast, Gran said.

Then we heard it. A long buzzing, throbbing, droning noise, a long way off and low in pitch, but rising gently as it came nearer. Planes! The sound droned on, getting louder. We heard the anti-aircraft guns in the park start up and then, suddenly, the first bomb fell with a dull 'crump' sound, some distance away, followed by another and another. Gran had just said, "Let's hope we're lucky tonight," when we heard a strange whistling sound, followed by a huge thud and a crash, and the whole house shook. "That must be just down the street," sighed Mum. A fire engine rushed by, its bell ringing furiously. "Incendiaries too," said Gran. After the bombing had stopped we huddled together in the dark for a long time listening to the night sounds. Eventually the 'all clear' sounded, much to our relief, and we dropped off to sleep to the sound of the kitchen clock.

MUSICAL ELEMENTS

All the elements

SPECIFIC OBJECTIVES

■ Composing a sound picture ■ Recording on tape ■ Evaluating and refining ideas ■ Devising a graphic score

KEY WORDS

Sequence, mood, musical technique

RESOURCES

■ CD 3 Track 14 'Sounds of the Blitz' ■ Photocopy Sheet 55 ■ Tape recorder ■ Any available instruments

Composing 'Blitz Night'

ACTIVITIES

■ *Composing a sound picture*

Give out Photocopy sheet 55 and read it through with the class. Explain that the task is to compose and record a picture in sound, telling this story without using any words. Somehow the sequence of sounds must not only tell the story but also convey to us the mood of the event and the feelings of the people involved.

Help the children to make a list showing the structure of the sound picture. It should have three columns, the first listing events in the story, the second the mood conveyed by the event and the third what musical techniques will help to convey these. The list might start like this:

Event	Mood	Musical techniques
The town at night	Mystery	Silence, quiet sounds, short, sharp timbres, thin texture

Play Track 14 and discuss the sounds with the children. **W❶**

Divide the class into groups of about six, divide the story into sections and give each group a section as their project. Allow them ten minutes to think up a sound sequence for their section. Review all the group work and, when they are ready, perform the whole sequence. Record this first attempt and review it for effectiveness when you listen to it together. Decide on ideas for improvement, and record the piece again.

WATCHPOINTS

W❶ *The sequence of sounds is: air raid siren, anti aircraft guns in distance, planes, bombs, fire engine (bell), more bombs, guns fading, all clear.*

FOLLOW UP

Set each group the task of recording graphically on paper their sequence of sounds. Display the work in the sequence in which it is heard. Let the groups work on and practise their sections to refine their work before recording the whole sequence on tape as a final version.

EXTENSION ACTIVITIES

One or two children may like to invent a piece of music of their own based on this story. Encourage them to invent it for whatever instrument they play, or to make a song.

SUPPORT ACTIVITIES

Involve every child in this sound-picture making, and keep a watchful eye on those who are less forthcoming in a group situation. Make certain that they have not been stuck with an instrument that will allow them no musical input to the group work.

ASSESSMENT POINTS

Make a note of those children who:
- choose appropriate sounds to match mood; • sequence sounds effectively; • evaluate and refine their ideas;
- can notate their music graphically.

Name ....

Date ....

Are you listening?
Band Music

You will hear six examples of instrumental music. Listen, and decide which group of instruments is playing.

1. orchestra   brass band   military band   swing band

2. orchestra   brass band   military band   swing band

3. orchestra   brass band   military band   swing band

4. orchestra   brass band   military band   swing band

5. orchestra   brass band   military band   swing band

6. orchestra   brass band   military band   swing band

MUSICAL ELEMENTS
Dynamics; Tempo; Timbre; Texture

SPECIFIC OBJECTIVES
■ Comparing two contrasting pieces of brass band music ■ Learning about brass and military bands ■ Distinguishing between different instrumental groups

KEY WORDS
Brass band, cornet, flugelhorn, percussion, woodwind, military band, orchestra

RESOURCES
■ CD 3 Track 15 Baker/Stone: *Ein Schnapps*; Track 16 Revaux et al: *My Way*; Track 17 'Are You Listening? Bands' ■ Photocopy Sheet 56
■ Poster 6

Listen to the Band

ACTIVITIES

■ *Listening and appraising*

Play Track 15 and ask the class to decide which instruments are playing the tune. *(The cornets.)* Help the children to identify the cornets on Poster 6. **W1**

Count how many cornet players there are. (Usually nine.) Explain that the cornets are the main focus of the band and usually play the most complicated music. **W2**

Draw attention to the flugelhorn on the poster, and play Track 16, which features a flugelhorn solo. Encourage the children to compare the two contrasting pieces. Focus on the difference in timbre between the cornet *(bright)* and the flugelhorn *(mellow)*, and the differences in tempo, dynamics and texture. Discuss the mood conveyed by the music, and help the children to realise the width of expressive sounds that a brass band can convey.

WATCHPOINTS

W1 *This would be a good opportunity to invite local brass band players to demonstrate and talk about their instruments.*

W2 *A brass band has only metal (brass) instruments in it, sometimes with percussion, but a military or marching band also includes woodwinds such as clarinets, flutes, piccolos and saxophones.*

FOLLOW UP
Use Track 17 and Photocopy sheet 56 to help the children distinguish between brass band, military band, and orchestra.
1. Spear: *Coronation Street* (brass band)
2. Sousa: *Sound Off* (military band)
3. Smyth: *The Wreckers Overture* (orchestra)
4. Traditional, arr. Finegan: *Little Brown Jug* (swing band)
5. Sousa: *The Royal Welch Fusiliers* (military band)
6. Offenbach: *The Can-Can* (brass band)

Completing the sheets will focus children's listening, and may give you some idea of how well they understand what they hear, but the most important part is the discussion afterwards. Encourage the children to discuss how the music makes them feel.

ASSESSMENT POINTS
Make a note of those children who:
- recognise the sound of a brass band; • can compare and contrast different brass band pieces; • can distinguish between different instrumental groups.

Summer Holiday

Words and music by Bruce Welch and B. Bennett

A We're all go-ing on a sum-mer hol-i-day

No more work-ing for a week or two——

Fun and laugh-ter on our sum-mer hol-i-day,

no more—— wor-ries for me or you,

B For a week—— or two. We're

go-ing where the sun shines bright-ly, We're

go-ing where the sea—— is blue. We've

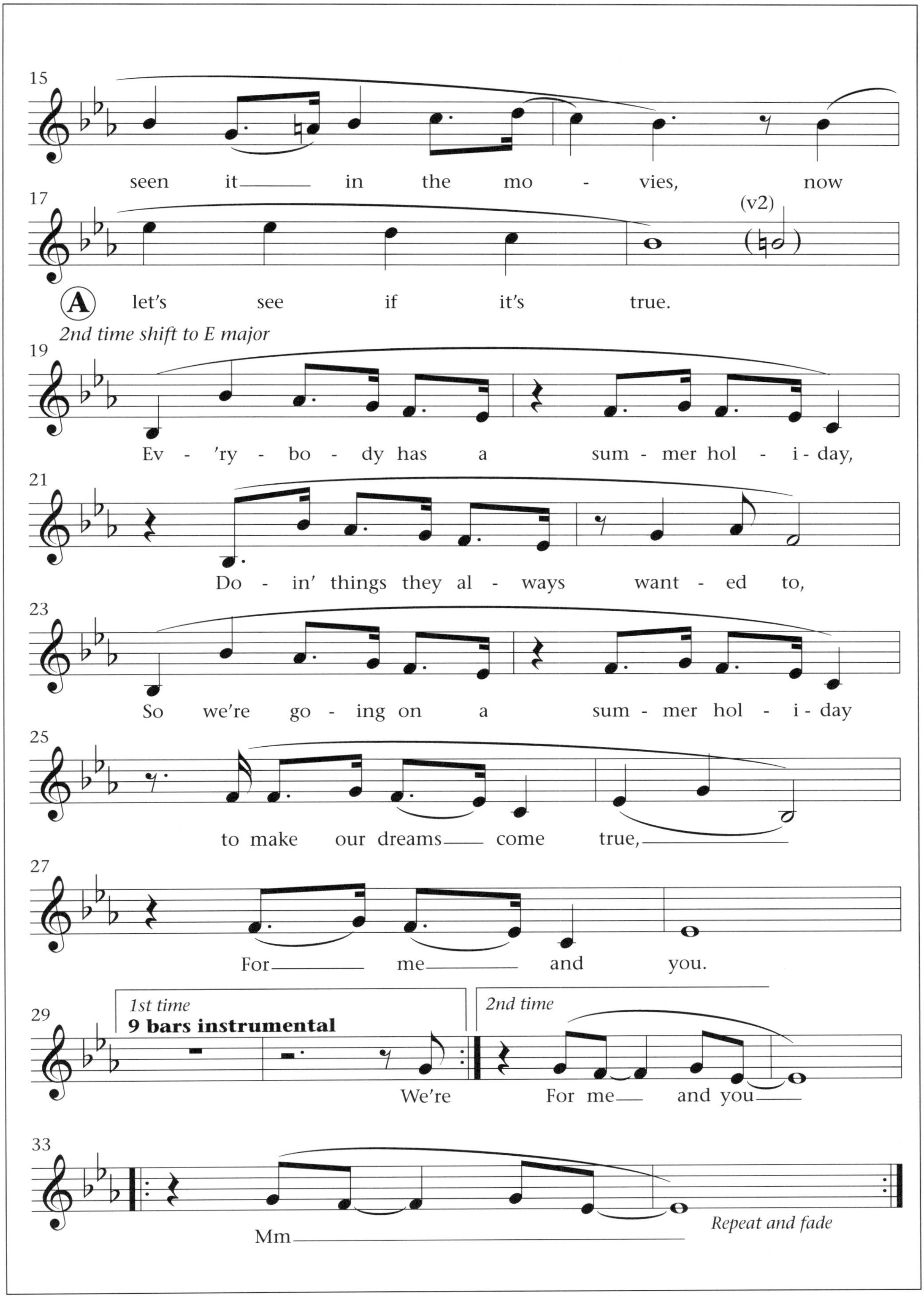
15
seen it in the mo - vies, now
17
(v2)
A let's see if it's true.
2nd time shift to E major
19
Ev - 'ry - bo - dy has a sum - mer hol - i - day,
21
Do - in' things they al - ways want - ed to,
23
So we're go - ing on a sum - mer hol - i - day
25
to make our dreams come true,
27
For me and you.
29
1st time
9 bars instrumental
We're
2nd time
For me and you
33
Mm
Repeat and fade

Summer Holiday

MUSICAL ELEMENTS
Duration; Timbre; Structure

SPECIFIC OBJECTIVES
- Experiencing 1960s pop music ■ Listening for structure
- Inventing new lyrics ■ Composing a holiday song

KEY WORDS
Pop, electric guitar, drum kit, phrase, middle eight, lyrics

RESOURCES
- CD 3 Track 18 'Summer Holiday' ■ Photocopy Sheets 57 and 58
- Any available instruments

ACTIVITIES

WATCHPOINTS

■ *Listening and appraising*

Play Track 18 and discuss the mood created by this song. *(Happy, relaxed.)* Ask: How is this atmosphere created? *(Strong beat at a medium tempo, jolly rhythm patterns, bright electric guitar timbre, crisp drum kit sound, light and sunny vocal timbre.)* **W1**

■ *Learning about pop song structure*

Ask the class to listen again for the structure of the song. Give out Photocopy sheets 57 and 58, play Track 18 again, and ask them to listen and look for phrases that repeat. *(Phrase 1 = phrase 3.)*

Discuss why this is called a 'pop' song. *(Short for 'popular')* Explain that most popular songs are structured in four bar phrases. **W2**

Help the children to hear how the structure balances by counting each bar as they listen again to the first part of the song, and notice how the composers add interest by adding an extra two bars at the end of the first eight bars ('For a week or two').

Draw attention to section B which provides a little contrast and a new idea in the lyrics. Explain that most popular songs have a B section, called a 'middle eight' (because it is usually eight bars long).

■ *Singing the song*

Encourage the class to sing with the recording as soon as they can.

W1 *This song was made famous by Cliff Richard in 1963 in the comedy film* Summer Holiday.

W2 *The phrases are marked and the bars are numbered in the notation.*

FOLLOW UP
Help the class to invent some song lyrics about a holiday or day out, to the melody and rhythm of 'Summer Holiday'. Help them to make certain that the middle eight has a contrasting idea and that it rhymes well. When you are all satisfied with your joint effort, let the class sing their version to the instrumental track, by turning the balance control to the right.

EXTENSION ACTIVITIES
Challenge more musically confident children to invent their own melody for your class song, or even better to invent a whole new song using the same structure and rhyme scheme. (It is sometimes difficult to invent new melodies for words that already have a known melody). If they are successful, encourage them to work out a performance routine, using unison dance movements, hand jives, etc., with or without instruments, and perform it to the class.

SUPPORT ACTIVITIES
Involve all the children in inventing a hand jive to this music. Hand jives first became popular in the 1950s and 1960s. Encourage the less musically confident to provide and demonstrate ideas for movements.

ASSESSMENT POINTS
Make a note of those children who:
- recognise a middle eight structure; • can invent new lyrics for a song; • can compose a song; • can invent a movement routine for a song.

MUSICAL ELEMENTS

Duration

SPECIFIC OBJECTIVES

■ Experiencing 1970s pop music ■ Moving to music in appropriate style ■ Responding to on and off beats

KEY WORDS

'On' beat and 'off beat'

RESOURCES

■ CD 3 Tracks 19 and 20 'Thank You for the Music' ■ Photocopy Sheets 59 and 60 ■ Space for movement

Thank You for the Music

ACTIVITIES

WATCHPOINTS

■ *Feeling the beat*

As a preparation to listening, ask the class to sit with their hands on their knees. Set up a strong beat on a drum and ask them to use first their right hands, and then their left to imitate it. Next ask them to alternate left and right. Then ask them to pat both knees and clap alternately. Help them to tell you that the pats are strong or 'on' beats and the claps weak or 'off' beats. Finally let them practise clicking their fingers only on the 'off' beat. **W❶**

W❶ *Unit 5 also includes work on on and off beats.*

■ *Listening to the song*

As the class listen to Track 20, ask them to sit quietly for the verse, listening to the story in the lyrics, and then join in with their off-beat finger clicks during the refrain. Encourage them to sing the refrain as soon as they can. Explain that the accompaniment in pop music usually accentuates the 'off' beat.

FOLLOW UP

In a space for movement, and taking suggestions from the children, work out with them a dance routine based on the refrain, with everyone making the same arm and leg movements in unison. All the movements should be on the 'off' beats. *(They could include pointing up to the right with the right hand, to the left with the left, hand jive gestures, step forward, back, etc.)*

Help them to learn the words of the verse and to stand and sing it in a line, performing their dance routine and singing the refrain.

EXTENSION ACTIVITIES

Give keen children a chance to invent their own special version of the routine and encourage them also to research ABBA costumes and to use dressing up materials to imitate them. Allow a chance for this performance to be seen and heard by others.

SUPPORT ACTIVITIES

If some children find clicking the 'off' beat too difficult, allow them just to join in with the beat as they feel it. They will probably imitate their peers, even if they do not understand the difference between 'off' and 'on' beats.

ASSESSMENT POINTS

Make a note of those children who:
  • understand the difference between on and off beats; • move on the off beat; • invent a dance routine.

Thank You For the Music

Benny Andersson and Bjorn Ulvaeus

Verse

Mo - ther says I___ was a dan - cer be - fore___ I could walk,

___ She says I be - gan___ to

sing long be - fore___ I could talk.___

And I've of - ten won - dered, how

did it all start,___ who found out that no - thing can

cap - ture a heart like a me - lo - dy can?___

Well who - ev - er it was,___ I'm a fan.___

Refrain

So I say thank you for the mu - sic, the

songs I'm sing - ing, Thanks for all the

joy they're bring - ing. Who can live with - out it? I

ask in all hon - es - ty, What would life be?

With - out a song or a dance, what are we?

So I say thank you for the mu - sic, for

1st and 2nd time

last time

giv- ing it to me. So I say giv-ing it to me.

This Is Our Country

George Odam

A

From the Chan - nel coast— to the north - ern high - lands,

Sing - ing as we tra - vel,— 'This is my— land!'—

From shore to shore, ov - er hill and val - ley,

Join us in this chor - us,— 'This is our home.'

B

Lake - land, moor - land, fen - land low,— The

spring that turns— in - to the riv - er's flow,—

This is our coun - try,   this is   our home,___

Cot - tage and cas - tle,   field___ and foam,___

A

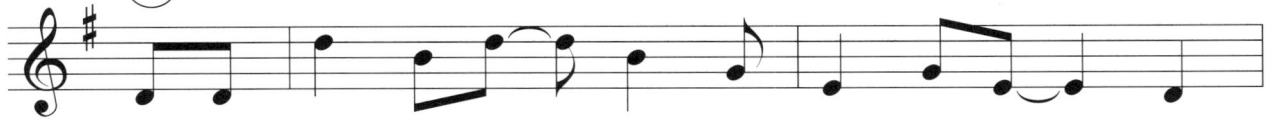

Ov - er   hill   and dale___ lies   the   road   be - fore___   us,

Sing - ing   as   we   tra - vel,___   'This   is   our home!'

This Is Our Country

MUSICAL ELEMENTS
Pitch; Duration; Timbre; Structure

SPECIFIC OBJECTIVES
■ Singing with expression ■ Inventing lyrics and melody for a new anthem ■ Notating, recording and performing a composed song

KEY WORDS
Verse, refrain, military band

RESOURCES
■ CD 3 Track 21 'This Is Our Country'; Track 22 'The National Anthem'
■ Non-pitched percussion instruments ■ Pitched percussion C D E G A C' ■ Photocopy Sheets 61 and 62 ■ Tape recorder

ACTIVITIES	WATCHPOINTS

■ *Listening to the song*

Give out Photocopy sheets 61 and 62, and ask the children to follow the words as they listen to Track 21. Discuss with them some of the places and things mentioned in the song. Encourage them to sing along when they can.

■ *Performing the song*

When they know the song well enough, help them to sing with enthusiasm. Insist on a good sitting position and encourage them to smile. Ask the children to add percussion instruments to a performance of this song (e.g. play the steady beat on a drum, play the strong first beat in every bar on a triangle or finger cymbals).

FOLLOW UP
Listen to Track 22, and ask the children if they recognise it. Explain that this is the British national anthem, and that it is representative of the whole country. Discuss when they might hear this music. (*At sporting events, on royal occasions.*) Ask: Why does it always start with a roll on the drums? (*As a warning, because it is traditional to stand up when this music is heard.*) You may wish to discuss other anthems, particularly if your own region/country has its own. ('You'll Never walk Alone' (CD2 Track 8) is an anthem of Liverpool FC.)

EXTENSION ACTIVITIES
Encourage the more able children to make up their own anthem. Ask: What are some of the things you might sing about? What are some of the things that make your own school, part of the country, town or village so special? When they have written the words, challenge them to invent a melody to go with them using C D E G A C' as the main pitches but adding others if they wish. Encourage composers to notate, record and perform their anthems.

SUPPORT ACTIVITIES
Help the least able children to learn the song by giving further opportunities to hear the recording. Help them to sing in time by providing a strong, steady beat on a drum or tambourine.

ASSESSMENT POINTS
Make a note of those children who:
- recognise the National Anthem;   • sing with expression;   • can play a steady beat;   • invent lyrics and melody for a new anthem and perform it.

Assessment for Unit 6

Using some aspects of the checklist below you may identify what the children are able to do when they have followed Unit 6.

MUSICAL ACTIVITIES

PERFORMING:

■ sing with expression;

■ sing with good breath control;

■ sing gently;

■ confidently maintain a second part;

■ play a steady beat.

COMPOSING:

■ sequence sounds effectively;

■ evaluate and refine ideas;

■ notate their music graphically;

■ compose a melody for a song;

■ invent a dance routine;

■ choose appropriate sounds to match mood;

■ invent new lyrics for a song;

■ invent a movement routine for a song;

■ invent lyrics and melody for a new anthem.

LISTENING AND APPRAISING:

■ identify and talk about a brass band;

■ distinguish between different instrumental groups;

■ comment on texture and timbre;

■ recognise a middle eight structure;

■ understand the difference between 'on' and 'off' beats;

■ move on the 'off' beat;

■ identify the structure of the song;

■ talk about the mood of the music;

■ understand how music reflects time and place;

■ compare and contrast different brass band pieces;

■ recognise the National Anthem.

Divali Song

UNIT 2 LESSON 3

George Odam

Call ... **Response**

Where the lights are twink - ling, Brave Prince Ra - ma comes.

Call ... **Response** ... **Call**

Can - dles by the hou - ses, Prin - cess Si - ta comes. From the dark - ness,

Response ... **Call** ... **Response**

Brave Prince Ra - ma comes. In - to bright - ness Prin - cess Si - ta comes.

Dona Nobis Pacem

UNIT 4 LESSON 1

Traditional
Piano arr. Philip Colls

123

Good News

UNIT 4 LESSON 4

Traditional Spiritual
Piano arr. Andrew Sackett

Good news, the char-iot's com-ing, Good news, the char-iot's com-ing, Good news, the char-iot's com-ing, And I don't want her leave-a me be-hind. Good news, Good news, the char-iot's com-ing Good news, Good news, the char-iot's com-ing, Good news, Good news, the

D7 Gm   B♭   E♭/F   B♭   E♭/F

char - iot's   com - ing,   And   I   don't want   her   leave - a   me,   Don't want   her   leave - a   me,

B♭   E♭/F   1.
                                     B♭   2.
                                                             E♭7   B♭6

Don't want   her   leave - a   me   be - hind.   hind.

Magic Bells

UNIT 4 LESSON 6

W. A. Mozart
Piano arr. Philip Colls

Oh— lis-ten to mu-sic that is charm-ing our ears. La la la la la la la la la la la la la. This— Mu-sic-al ma-gic from no-where ap-pears. La la la la la la la la la la la la la. la.

D.S. for introduction to verse 2 and Coda (al Fine)

Mistletoe and Wine

UNIT 2 LESSON 6

Leslie Stewart, Jeremy Paul
and Keith Strachan

Verses colla voce

1. The

child is a— king, the car - oll - ers— sing, The old is

passed, there's a new——— be - gin - ning. Dreams of San - ta,

A
B⁷sus⁽⁹⁾
E⁷

dreams of snow, Fin - gers numb, fac - es a - glow. It's

Refrain
A

Christ - mas time, mis - tle - toe and wine, Child - ren

D   A   E   E⁷

sing - ing Chris - ti - an rhyme With logs on the fire—— and

gifts on the tree; A time to re - joice in the good that we see. 2. A
3. It's a

A

time———— for liv - ing, a time for be - liev - ing, A
time———— for giv - ing, a time for get - ting, A

time for trusting, not de-ceiv-ing.
time for for-giv-ing, and for for-get-ting.

Love and laugh-ter and joy ev-er af-ter;
Christ-mas is love, Christ-mas is peace;

Ours for the tak-ing just fol-low the mas-ter.
time for hat-ing and fight-ing to cease.

Christ-mas time, mis-tle-toe and wine, child-ren sing-ing

Chris-ti-an rhyme With logs on the fire and gifts on the tree;

time to re-joice in the good that we see. see.

Music's Mine

UNIT 5 LESSON 5

George Odam

Mu - sic, mu - sic, mu - sic sur-rounds us, har - mo - ny, mel - o - dy and rhy - thm com - bine,— Mu - sic, mu - sic, mu - sic a - round— us, when we play or we sing— we're feel - ing fine. Har - mo - ny, mel - o - dy, rhy - thm, tex - ture and struc - ture mak - ing Mu - sic, mu - sic, mu - sic a - bound - ing all the day long,— sing - ing a song,— Sing - ing it strong - ly for mu - sic's mine!

Notin' Around

UNIT 1 LESSON 3

Shena Power
Piano arr. Philip Colls

Section 4

we can sing it round and round. When you're in a hur-ry then the

Am ... D7

eighth notes are the best, be-cause they simp-ly keep on run-ning and you

G ... G

nev-er take a rest, And you can tra-vel up and down the scale with

Am ... D7

el-e-gance and ease, and if you don't de-cide to stop in time you'll

Section 5

G ... G ... Am ... D7

end up on your knees! It's sound ed-u-ca-tion to add syn-co-

G ... G ... Am ... D7 ... G

pa-tion. Just swing in-to ac-tion to jazz up this song!

Now Light
One Thousand Christmas Lights

UNIT 2 LESSON 4

Folk song from Sweden
Arranged by George Odam

1. Now light one thou-sand Christ-mas lights On dark earth here to - night; One

thou-sand, thou - sand al - so shine To make the dark sky bright.

Polish the Old Menorah

UNIT 2 LESSON 1

Joan K. Arnold

Refrain

Po - lish the old Me - no - rah, Cha - nu - kah's here a - gain!

Can - dles we light one for each night.

Can - dles we light one for each

Cha - nu - kah's here a - gain. *Fine*

night here a - gain.

Much Faster

1. Once u - pon a time there was war there was fight - ing.

Fight - ing for the tem - ple with sling and with sword.

Ju - das Mac - a - bee and his brave band of sol - diers

fought a - gainst the Syr - ians in praise of the Lord.

rit. -

Silver Moon

UNIT 1 LESSON 6

Anon.
Piano arr. Philip Colls

Introduction

Descant

Voice lyrics:
Oh Sil - ver Moon, Moon,

bright and shin - y moon, Won't you please shine down on me?— Oh Sil - ver

Moon, Moon bright and shin - y moon Won't you come from be - hind that

Moon, Moon, bright and shin - y moon, Won't you come from be - hind that

Vocal/lyric line (top staff): tree? Hoo,

Piano: tree? Oh, my heart is bump-ing and I'm scared to see, There's a

D   D⁷   G

C   C♯dim   D⁷   G   Em⁷

hoo, Oh Moon, Moon,

creep-y sha-dow hang-ing ov-er me, Oh Sil-ver Moon, Moon,

A   D   G

bright and shin-y moon, Won't you please shine down on me?

bright and shin-y moon, Won't you please shine down on me?

CODA

C   C♯dim   G   E⁷   D   G

Simple Gifts

UNIT 3 LESSON 1

Traditional Shaker song
Piano arr. Andrew Sackett

'Tis the gift to be sim-ple, 'tis the gift to be free, 'Tis the gift to come down where you ought to be, And when we find our-selves in the place just right, It-'ll be in the val-ley of love and de-light. When true sim-pli-ci-ty is gained, To

138

Gm   C   F

bow   and   to   bend   we   shan't   be   a-shamed,   To   turn,   turn   will

D⁷   Gm   C⁷   F   B♭

be   our   de - light,   Till   by   turn - ing,   turn - ing   we   come   out

1.   2.   G⁷   C⁷   F   B♭   F
F   F

right   right.

Songs of the West

Compilation of Rock Island Line, Midnight Special and Worried Man

UNIT 3 LESSON 6

Traditional songs arranged by Brian Ley
Piano arr. Andrew Sackett

Rock Island Line
Refrain

Oh the Rock Is-land Line— is a

migh-ty good road,— Well the Rock Is-land Line— is the road to ride,— Oh the

Rock Is-land Line— is a migh-ty good road,— If you want— to ride it, got to

ride it like you find it, Get your tick-et at the sta-tion on the Rock Is-land Line.—

Verse

1. Train's com-in' down the track, run-nin' real well, Blow-in' the whis-tle and
2. Train's left St Lou-is at quar-ter to nine, Got to Fort Worth— for

Refrain

ring-in' the bell.— Oh the Rock Is-land Line— is a migh-ty good road,— Well the
din - ner time.—

Rock Is-land Line— is the road to ride,— Oh the Rock Is-land Line— is a

migh-ty good road,— If you want— to ride it, got to ride it like you find it, Get your

tick - et at the sta-tion on the Rock Is-land Line.—

Midnight Special

Let the Mid-night Spe - cial— shine its light on

me,— Let the Mid-night Spe - cial—

141

Worried Man

shine its ev-er-lov-in' light on me. It takes a wor-ried

man to sing a wor-ried song, It takes a wor-ried man to

sing a wor-ried song, It takes a wor-ried man to sing a wor-ried

song, I'm wor-ried now, but I won't be wor-ried long. The

train I ride is six-teen coa-ches long, The train I ride is

six-teen coa-ches long, The train I ride is six-teen coa-ches

142

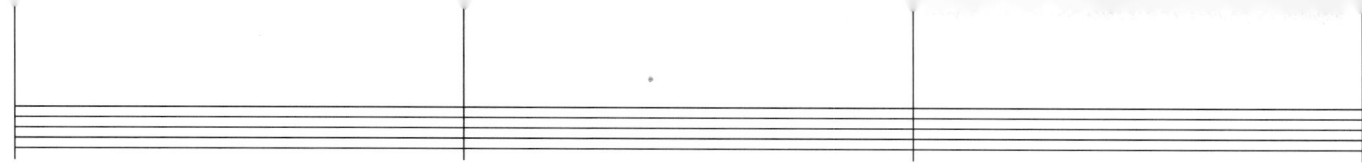

long, But the one I love____ was on that train and gone. It

takes a wor-ried man to sing a wor-ried song, It takes a wor-ried

man to sing a wor-ried song, It takes a wor-ried man to

sing a wor-ried song, I'm wor-ried now, but I won't be wor-ried long,

I'm wor-ried now, but I won't be wor-ried long.____

Summer Holiday

UNIT 6 LESSON 5

Bruce Welch and B. Bennett
Piano arr. Philip Colls

Introduction

We're all go - ing on a sum - mer hol - i-day No more work-ing for a

week or two— Fun and laugh - ter on our sum - mer hol - i-day,

no more— wor - ries for me or you, For a week— or

two. We're go - ing where the sun shines bright - ly, We're

go-ing where the sea— is blue. We've seen it—— in the mo - vies, now

let's see if it's true. We're all go - ing on a sum - mer hol - i - day

No more work-ing for a week or two— Fun and laugh-ter on our

sum-mer hol - i - day, no more— wor - ries for me or you,

Interlude

For a week— or two.

145

We're go-ing where the sun shines bright-ly, We're

go-ing where the sea__ is blue We've seen it__ in the mov - ies, now

let's see if it's true Ev - 'ry - bo - dy has a sum - mer hol - i - day,

Do - in' things they al - ways want-ed to, __ So we're go - ing on a

sum - mer hol - i - day to make our dreams come true_____ For__ me__ and

you. For me_ and you__ Mm_____

146

Syncopation

UNIT 5 LESSON 1

George Odam
Piano arr. Andrew Sackett

Syn - co - pa - ted rhy-thm gets— us danc - ing; hands— and feet are tap-ping, it's— en - tran - cing. Fas - cin - a - tion 'cross— the na - tion. Ev - ry-one loves syn - co - pa - tion.—

Can you hear those dan - cing feet tap - ping to the beat with syn-co - pa - tion? Syn-co - pa - tion, syn - co - pa - tion, ev' - ry-one dan - cing to the beat. Syn - co - pa - tion!

Thank You For the Music

UNIT 6 LESSON 6

Benny Andersson and Bjorn Ulvaeus
Piano arr. Andrew Sackett

Mo - ther says I___ was a dan - cer be - fore___ I could walk,___ She says I be - gan___ to sing long be - fore___ I could talk.___ And I've of - ten won - dered, how did it all start, who found out that no - thing can cap - ture a heart___ like a me - lo - dy can?___

Well who-ev - er it was, I'm a fan. So I say

thank you for the mu - sic, the songs I'm sing-ing, Thanks for all the

joy ther're bring-ing. Who can live with-out it? I ask in all hon-es-ty,

What would life be? With-out a song or a dance, what are we?

So I say thank you for the mu - sic, for giv-ing it to me.

So I say giv-ing it to me.

The Inch Worm

UNIT 1 LESSON 1

Frank Loesser
Piano arr. Philip Colls

Introduction

Two and two are four, four and four are eight,

That's all you have on your bus' - ness - like mind.

Two and two are four, four and four are eight,

How can you be so blind?_____

Descant

F · Eb7 · F · Eb7

Two and two are four, four and four are eight,

F · Bb · Bbm · F · C

Eight and eight are six - teen, six - teen and six - teen are thir - ty - two.

F · Eb7 · F · Eb7

(Two and two are four,) (four and four are eight,)

Inch - worm, Inch - worm, mea - sur - ing the mar - i - golds,

F · Bb · Bbm · F · G7 · C

(Eight and eight are six - teen, six - teen and six - teen are thir - ty - two.)

You and your a - rith - me - tic, you'll prob - a - bly go far. _____

F · Eb7 · F · Eb7

(Two and two are four,) (four and four are eight,)

Inch - worm, Inch - worm, mea - sur - ing the mar - i - golds,

F · Bb · Bbm · F · C · F

(Eight and eight are six - teen, six - teen and six - teen are thir - ty - two.)

Seems to me you'd stop and see how beau - ti - ful they are.

(**CODA** – repeat last 4 bars)

151

The White Cliffs of Dover

UNIT 6 LESSON 2

Nat Burton and Walter Kent
Piano arr. Philip Colls

Introduction

Verse

I'll nev-er for-get the peo-ple I met brav-ing those an - gry skies; I re-

mem - ber well as the sha-dows fell, The light of hope in their eyes. And

tho' I'm far a-way, I still can hear them say, 'Thumbs up!' For when the

Refrain

dawn comes up: There'll be Blue-birds ov - er the white cliffs of Dov-er, to -

Dm⁷ — **G⁷** — **C** — **Am** — **Dm** — **G⁷** — **C** — **Em** — **C⁷**

mor - row, just you wait and see There'll be love and laugh - ter and

F — **C** — **Am** — **Dm⁷** — **G⁷** — **C** — **F** — **C** — **C⁷**

peace ev - er af - ter, to - mor - row, when the world is free._____ The

F — **F♯dim⁷** — **C** — **(C)** — **C⁷**

shep - herd will tend his sheep, The val - ley will bloom a - gain, And

F — **Dm** — **Am** — **D** — **G**

Jim - my will go to sleep in his own lit - tle room a - gain. There'll be

C — **Em** — **C⁷** — **F** — **C** — **Am** — **Dm⁷**

Blue - birds ov - er the white cliffs of Do - ver, to - mor - row,

G⁷ — *1.* **C** — **C⁷** — **Dm** — **G⁷** — *2.* **C** — **Fm** — **C**

just you wait and see._____ see._____

153

This Is Our Country

UNIT 6 LESSON 7

George Odam

Lyrics:

From the Chan - nel coast — to the north - ern high - lands, Sing - ing as we tra - vel, — 'This is my — land!' — From shore to shore, — ov - er hill and val - ley, Join us in this chor - us, — 'This is our home.' Lake - land, moor - land, fen - land low, — The spring that turns — in - to the riv - er's flow, — This is our coun - try, this is our home, — Cot - tage and cas - tle, field and farm — Ov - er hill and dale — lies the road be - fore — us, Sing - ing as we tra - vel, — 'This is our home!'

Turn, turn, turn

UNIT 1 LESSON 7

Pete Seeger
Piano arr. Philip Colls

Introduction

To ev - 'ry - thing (Turn, turn, turn,) There

is a season (Turn, turn, turn) And a time for ev - 'ry pur - pose un - der heav - en.

Fine
(last time)
(last time)

Verse

1. A time to be born, a time— to die; A time to plant, a time— to
2. A time to— gain, a time— to lose; A time to rend a time— to

reap; A time to kill, a time— to heal; A time to laugh, a time to
mend; A time to love, a time— to hate; A time for peace, it's not too

1.
weep.— To ev - 'ry

2.
late.— To ev - 'ry

155

We're Going to the Country

UNIT 6 LESSON 1

Lionel Bart
Piano arr. Philip Colls

Extra voice part (like a descant)

Look af-ter your-self, Sid-dy, look af-ter your-

We're go - ing to the coun - try,

R.H.

Octave lower (optional)

self   Look af - ter your-self,   Tom - my, look af - ter you -

We're going   to see   the cows.

self   Eat three meals a day,   ev - 'ry day

We're going to have a real bath   in a love - ly

156

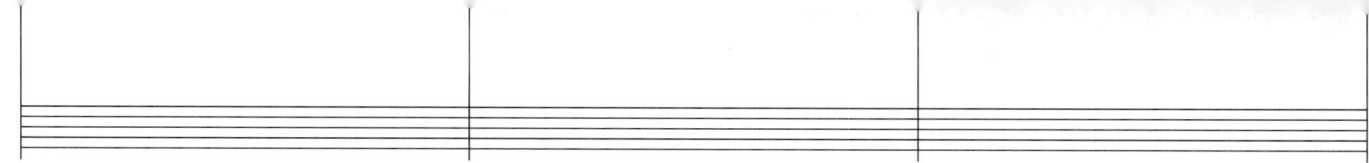

Please don't cry while you're a - way____ Look af - ter your-self, Tom-my, look af - ter your-self.

house   They call it 'va - cu - a - tion

Look af - ter your-self, Cath - y, look af - ter your-self.

They take you to the sta - tion

Bye - bye,   Bye - bye

They put you on a train   Let's hope it does - n't rain.   We're go - ing to the

CODA

Bye - bye.

coun - try

Work-a-day Mornin' Blues

UNIT 3 LESSON 3

Music by Sol Berkowitz
Words by Rosemary Jacques
Piano arr. Andrew Sackett

Lyrics:

1. I'm wear-y of ris-in' at break of day,— And hav-in' my chores to do,— I'm wear-y of ris-in' at break of day,— And hav-in' my chores to do.— 'Cause I've got me those— work-a-day morn-in' blues.— 2. I'd

3. Got to chase away those— work-a-day morn-in' blues.

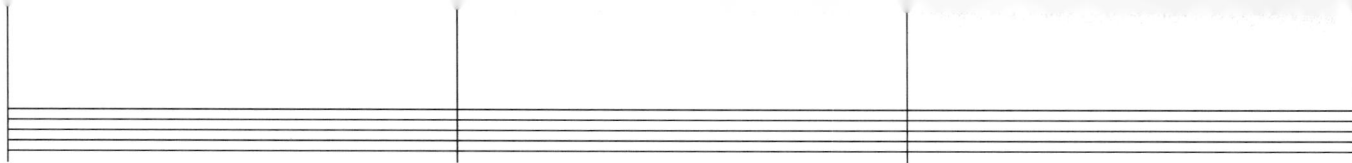

Work - a - day   blues.

You'll Never Walk Alone

UNIT 3 LESSON 5

Words by Oscar Hammerstein II
Music by Richard Rogers
Piano arr. Andrew Sackett

Lyrics under the staves:

When you walk through a storm, hold your head up high And don't be a-fraid of the dark. At the end of the storm is a gold - en sky And the sweet sil - ver song of a lark. Walk on through the wind, Walk

	PERFORMING				COMPOSING			
Pupils should be given opportunities to:	**a** Control sounds made by the voice and a range of tuned and untuned instruments.	**b** Perform with others, and develop awareness of audience, venue and occasion.			**c** Compose in response to variety of stimuli, and explore a range of resources e.g. voices, instruments, sounds from the environment.	**d** Communicate musical ideas to others.		
Pupils should be taught to:	**a** sing songs, developing control of diction and musical elements, particularly phrasing, eg giving shape to a song by breathing at the end of a phrase;	**b** play pieces and accompaniments and perform musical patterns by ear and from notations, eg symbols which define musical elements, with increasing dexterity and control;	**c** sing songs, including songs and rounds in two parts, and play pieces which have several parts, developing the ability to listen to the other performers;	**d** rehearse and present their own projects/performances;	**e** improvise rhythmic and melodic ideas, eg add a percussion part to a song;	**f** explore, create, select, combine and organise sounds in musical structures, eg using repeated sections or verse and chorus;	**g** use sounds and structures to achieve an intended effect, eg to create a particular atmosphere;	**h** refine and record their compositions using notation(s), where appropriate.
UNIT 1								
1 Inch Worm	✓		✓	✓				
2 Composing a Slow Waltz		✓		✓	✓	✓		✓
3 Notin' Around	✓	✓	✓	✓		✓		
4 Concertos								
5 Weaving Melodies		✓		✓	✓	✓	✓	✓
6 Silver Moon	✓	✓	✓	✓	✓			
7 Turn, Turn	✓	✓	✓	✓				
UNIT 2								
1 Polish The Old Menorah	✓	✓	✓	✓	✓			
2 Composing in Layers		✓	✓	✓	✓	✓		✓
3 Divali Song	✓	✓	✓		✓	✓		✓
4 Now Light 1000	✓		✓	✓				
5 AYL? Christmas								
6 Mistletoe and Wine	✓	✓	✓	✓	✓			✓
UNIT 3								
1 Simple Gifts	✓	✓	✓	✓				
2 Porgy & Bess								
3 The Blues	✓	✓	✓	✓	✓	✓	✓	✓
4 Heal the Soul				✓	✓	✓	✓	✓
5 You'll Never Walk Alone	✓		✓	✓				
6 Songs of the West	✓	✓	✓	✓	✓			
7 Making a Blues Song	✓	✓	✓	✓	✓	✓	✓	✓
UNIT 4								
1 Dona Nobis Pacem	✓		✓	✓				
2 Sumer Is Icumen In	✓	✓	✓	✓		✓		
3 AYL? Farandole		✓		✓	✓	✓		✓
4 Good News	✓	✓	✓	✓	✓			
5 Operetta								
6 Mozart's Magic Bells	✓	✓	✓	✓		✓	✓	
UNIT 5								
1 Syncopation	✓	✓	✓	✓	✓			
2 African Chant	✓	✓	✓	✓				
3 Song for Oxum	✓	✓	✓			✓	✓	
4 AYL? Syncopation								
5 Music's Mine	✓		✓	✓				
6 Improvising		✓		✓	✓	✓	✓	✓
UNIT 6								
1 We're going to the Country	✓		✓	✓				
2 White Cliffs of Dover	✓		✓	✓			✓	
3 Blitz Night		✓		✓		✓	✓	✓
4 Listen to the Band								
5 Summer Holiday	✓		✓	✓	✓	✓	✓	✓
6 Thank You for the Music	✓	✓	✓	✓	✓			
7 This Is Our Country	✓	✓	✓	✓	✓	✓	✓	✓

LISTENING

e Listen to, and develop understanding of, music from different times and places, applying knowledge to their own work.

APPRAISING

f Respond to and evaluate live performances and recorded music, including their own and others' compositions and performances.

MUSICAL ELEMENTS

a identify the sounds made by a variety of instruments individually and in combination, eg classroom instruments and families of instruments;	b identify how musical elements and resources, eg voices, instruments, performers, can be used to communicate a mood or effect;	c recognise ways in which music reflects the time and place in which it is created;	d compare music from contrasting musical traditions, and respond to differences in character and mood, eg through dance or other suitable forms of expression;	e express ideas and opinions about music, developing a musical vocabulary and the ability to use musical knowledge to support views.	Pitch	Duration	Dynamics	Tempo	Timbre	Texture	Structure
	✓		✓	✓	✓	✓	✓	✓	✓	✓	
				✓	✓	✓		✓			
				✓		✓			✓	✓	✓
✓	✓	✓	✓	✓					✓	✓	
				✓	✓					✓	✓
				✓	✓					✓	
	✓		✓	✓	✓				✓	✓	
	✓	✓	✓	✓			✓	✓		✓	✓
				✓	✓	✓	✓	✓	✓	✓	✓
	✓		✓	✓	✓	✓					✓
	✓		✓	✓		✓			✓		✓
✓	✓	✓	✓	✓					✓	✓	✓
✓	✓	✓	✓	✓		✓			✓	✓	
✓	✓	✓	✓	✓	✓	✓	✓	✓	✓	✓	✓
✓	✓	✓	✓	✓					✓		
	✓	✓	✓	✓	✓	✓				✓	
✓	✓	✓	✓	✓	✓	✓	✓	✓	✓	✓	✓
	✓	✓	✓	✓	✓		✓		✓		✓
			✓	✓	✓	✓		✓		✓	✓
	✓	✓		✓	✓	✓				✓	✓
	✓			✓	✓		✓			✓	✓
		✓	✓	✓	✓				✓	✓	
✓	✓	✓	✓	✓	✓	✓	✓	✓	✓		
	✓	✓	✓	✓	✓	✓	✓	✓	✓	✓	
✓	✓	✓	✓	✓	✓				✓	✓	✓
✓	✓	✓	✓	✓					✓	✓	✓
	✓	✓	✓	✓		✓					✓
	✓	✓	✓	✓		✓					✓
✓	✓	✓	✓	✓	✓	✓			✓		
	✓	✓	✓	✓		✓					
				✓	✓	✓	✓	✓	✓		✓
✓	✓	✓	✓	✓	✓	✓			✓	✓	
	✓	✓	✓	✓					✓	✓	✓
	✓	✓	✓	✓							✓
	✓	✓	✓	✓	✓	✓	✓	✓	✓	✓	✓
✓	✓	✓	✓	✓				✓	✓	✓	✓
✓	✓	✓	✓	✓		✓			✓		✓
			✓	✓		✓				✓	
✓	✓	✓	✓	✓	✓	✓			✓		✓

Pupils should be taught to:	**PERFORMING**							
	a imitate rhythms and melodies; memorise, internalise (hear in their heads) and recall musical patterns and songs;	**b** perform from signals and/or written symbols and respond to a variety of musical instructions;	**c** sing an expanding repertoire of songs (unison and simple two-part), and pieces requiring a variety of vocal techniques, with increasing control of breathing, diction, phrasing and dynamics and accuracy of pitch and duration;	**d** perform pieces/accompaniments on a widening range of instruments, using appropriate playing techniques and with increasing dexterity and control of sound;	**e** maintain a part as a member of a group in a simple part song;	**f** play an individual instrumental part in a group piece;	**g** rehearse and take increasing responsibility in preparing for performances;	**h** plan and present their own performances, being aware of the need to communicate to different audiences.
UNIT 1								
1 Inch Worm	✓		✓		✓		✓	
2 Composing a Slow Waltz	✓	✓		✓		✓	✓	
3 Notin' Around	✓	✓	✓	✓	✓	✓	✓	✓
4 Concertos								
5 Weaving Melodies	✓	✓		✓		✓	✓	
6 Silver Moon	✓	✓	✓	✓	✓	✓	✓	
7 Turn, Turn	✓	✓	✓	✓	✓	✓	✓	✓
UNIT 2								
1 Polish The Old Menorah	✓		✓	✓	✓	✓	✓	
2 Composing in Layers	✓	✓		✓		✓	✓	
3 Divali Song	✓	✓	✓	✓	✓	✓	✓	
4 Now Light 1000	✓	✓	✓				✓	
5 AYL? Christmas								
6 Mistletoe and Wine	✓	✓	✓	✓	✓	✓	✓	
UNIT 3								
1 Simple Gifts	✓	✓	✓	✓		✓	✓	
2 Porgy & Bess								
3 The Blues	✓	✓	✓			✓	✓	
4 Heal the Soul				✓		✓		
5 You'll Never Walk Alone	✓	✓	✓				✓	
6 Songs of the West	✓	✓	✓	✓	✓	✓	✓	
7 Making a Blues Song	✓	✓	✓	✓		✓	✓	
UNIT 4								
1 Dona Nobis Pacem	✓		✓		✓		✓	
2 Sumer Is Icumen In	✓	✓	✓	✓	✓	✓	✓	
3 AYL? Farandole	✓			✓		✓	✓	✓
4 Good News	✓	✓	✓	✓	✓	✓	✓	
5 Operetta								
6 Mozart's Magic Bells	✓	✓	✓	✓	✓	✓	✓	
UNIT 5								
1 Syncopation	✓	✓	✓	✓	✓	✓	✓	
2 African Chant	✓	✓	✓	✓	✓	✓	✓	
3 Song for Oxum	✓	✓	✓	✓		✓	✓	
4 AYL? Syncopation								
5 Music's Mine	✓	✓	✓		✓		✓	
6 Improvising		✓		✓		✓	✓	
UNIT 6								
1 We're Going to the Country	✓	✓	✓		✓		✓	✓
2 White Cliffs of Dover	✓		✓				✓	✓
3 Blitz Night		✓		✓		✓	✓	✓
4 Listen to the Band								
5 Summer Holiday	✓	✓	✓			✓	✓	✓
6 Thank You for the Music	✓	✓	✓				✓	✓
7 This Is Our Country	✓	✓	✓				✓	✓

	COMPOSING					APPRAISING			MUSICAL ELEMENTS							
	a explore and use a widening range of sound sources including their voices, bodies, sounds from the environment and instruments;	b create, select and organise sounds to produce a specific mood or atmosphere;	c improvise, compose and arrange music in response to a range of musical and extra-musical stimuli, using appropriate structures;	d develop and refine musical ideas;	e communicate their ideas using recording equipment, signs and symbols, or cues.	a listen attentively to their own and others' music in order to distinguish differences within the musical elements;	b listen attentively to music of different styles, times and cultures, and identify its main characteristics;	c describe, discuss and evaluate music, including their own compositions and performances.	Pitch	Duration	Pace (tempo)	Timbre	Texture	Dynamics	Structure	Silence
						✓	✓	✓	✓	✓	✓	✓	✓	✓		
	✓	✓	✓	✓	✓	✓		✓	✓	✓	✓					
	✓	✓	✓	✓	✓	✓		✓		✓		✓	✓		✓	
						✓	✓	✓				✓	✓			
	✓		✓	✓	✓	✓		✓	✓				✓		✓	
	✓		✓			✓		✓	✓				✓			
			✓			✓	✓	✓	✓			✓			✓	
			✓			✓	✓	✓		✓		✓	✓	✓		
	✓		✓	✓	✓	✓		✓	✓	✓	✓	✓	✓	✓	✓	✓
			✓	✓	✓	✓	✓	✓	✓	✓					✓	✓
	✓					✓		✓		✓		✓			✓	✓
						✓	✓	✓				✓	✓		✓	
	✓	✓	✓	✓		✓	✓	✓				✓	✓			
						✓	✓	✓	✓	✓	✓	✓	✓	✓	✓	
						✓	✓	✓				✓				
	✓		✓	✓		✓	✓	✓	✓	✓		✓				
	✓	✓	✓	✓	✓	✓	✓	✓	✓	✓	✓	✓	✓	✓	✓	✓
						✓	✓	✓	✓			✓		✓	✓	
			✓			✓	✓	✓	✓	✓	✓		✓		✓	✓
			✓	✓	✓	✓		✓	✓	✓			✓		✓	
						✓		✓	✓				✓	✓	✓	✓
			✓		✓	✓	✓	✓	✓			✓			✓	
			✓	✓		✓	✓	✓	✓	✓	✓	✓	✓	✓	✓	✓
						✓	✓	✓	✓			✓	✓		✓	
	✓	✓				✓	✓	✓	✓							
						✓	✓	✓	✓						✓	
			✓		✓	✓	✓	✓	✓	✓		✓			✓	
	✓	✓				✓	✓	✓	✓	✓		✓				
						✓	✓	✓	✓							
						✓		✓	✓	✓	✓	✓	✓			✓
	✓	✓	✓	✓	✓	✓	✓	✓	✓	✓		✓	✓			
						✓	✓	✓				✓	✓		✓	✓
		✓				✓	✓	✓							✓	
	✓	✓	✓	✓	✓	✓		✓	✓	✓	✓	✓	✓	✓	✓	✓
						✓	✓	✓		✓		✓	✓	✓		
		✓	✓	✓	✓	✓		✓		✓		✓			✓	
				✓		✓	✓	✓		✓						
		✓	✓	✓	✓	✓	✓	✓	✓	✓		✓			✓	

165

Attainment Outcomes Levels C/D — Strands	Using materials, techniques, skills and media			Expressing feelings, ideas, thoughts and solutions		Evaluating and appreciating	Concepts						
	Investigating: exploring sound	Using the voice	Using instruments	Creating and designing	Communicating and presenting	Observing, listening, reflecting, describing and responding	Pitch	Rhythm/Pulse	Dynamics	Tempo	Tone (timbre)	Texture	Form (structure)
UNIT 1													
1 Inch Worm		✓				✓	✓	✓	✓	✓	✓	✓	
2 Composing a Slow Waltz			✓	✓	✓	✓	✓	✓		✓			
3 Notin' Around		✓	✓	✓	✓	✓		✓			✓	✓	✓
4 Concertos						✓					✓	✓	
5 Weaving Melodies	✓		✓	✓	✓	✓	✓					✓	✓
6 Silver Moon		✓	✓	✓	✓	✓	✓					✓	
7 Turn, Turn		✓	✓	✓	✓	✓	✓				✓	✓	✓
UNIT 2													
1 Polish the Old Menorah		✓	✓	✓		✓			✓	✓	✓	✓	✓
2 Composing in Layers			✓	✓	✓	✓	✓	✓	✓	✓	✓	✓	✓
3 Divali song		✓	✓	✓	✓	✓	✓	✓					✓
4 Now Light 1000		✓			✓	✓		✓			✓		✓
5 AYL? Christmas						✓					✓	✓	✓
6 Mistletoe and Wine		✓	✓	✓	✓	✓		✓			✓		
UNIT 3													
1 Simple Gifts		✓	✓	✓	✓	✓	✓	✓	✓	✓	✓	✓	✓
2 Porgy & Bess						✓					✓		
3 The Blues	✓	✓	✓	✓	✓	✓	✓	✓				✓	
4 Heal the Soul	✓	✓	✓	✓	✓	✓	✓	✓	✓	✓	✓	✓	✓
5 You'll Never Walk Alone		✓			✓	✓	✓		✓		✓		✓
6 Songs of the West		✓	✓	✓	✓	✓	✓	✓			✓		✓
7 Making a Blues Song	✓	✓	✓	✓	✓	✓	✓	✓			✓		✓
UNIT 4													
1 Dona Nobis Pacem		✓			✓	✓	✓		✓		✓	✓	
2 Sumer Is Icumen In		✓	✓	✓	✓	✓	✓	✓			✓	✓	
3 AYL? Farandole			✓	✓	✓	✓	✓	✓	✓	✓	✓	✓	✓
4 Good News		✓	✓	✓	✓	✓	✓	✓	✓	✓	✓	✓	✓
5 Operetta						✓	✓				✓	✓	✓
6 Mozart's Magic Bells	✓	✓	✓	✓	✓	✓					✓	✓	✓
UNIT 5													
1 Syncopation		✓	✓	✓	✓	✓		✓					✓
2 African Chorus		✓	✓		✓	✓		✓					
3 Song for Oxum	✓	✓	✓	✓	✓	✓	✓	✓			✓		
4 AYL? Syncopation						✓		✓					
5 Music's Mine		✓			✓	✓	✓	✓	✓	✓	✓	✓	✓
6 Improvising	✓		✓	✓	✓	✓	✓	✓			✓	✓	
UNIT 6													
1 We're Going to the Country		✓			✓	✓					✓	✓	✓
2 White Cliffs of Dover		✓				✓					✓		✓
3 Blitz Night	✓		✓	✓	✓	✓	✓	✓	✓	✓	✓	✓	✓
4 Listen to the Band						✓			✓	✓	✓	✓	
5 Summer Holiday		✓	✓	✓	✓	✓		✓			✓		✓
6 Thank You for the Music		✓		✓	✓	✓		✓					
7 This Is Our Country		✓	✓	✓	✓	✓	✓	✓			✓		✓

Using classroom musical instruments

This section shows a selection of the pitched and non-pitched percussion instruments which are most likely to be found in primary schools. It identifies the instruments and suggests ways in which to play them. Children should be encouraged to play the instruments correctly and with good control in order to produce the best sound quality. They should also be given opportunities to experiment with the instruments, playing them in a less conventional way, exploring the full range of sounds which they can produce.

Pitched instruments should have medium or large sized bars. Have a good selection of different beaters for all instruments so that various timbres (sound colours) can be produced.

PITCHED INSTRUMENTS

■ *Chime Bars, Xylophone, Glockenspiel*
  • Hold beaters as illustrated and bounce in the middle of the bar.
  • Use hand to stop the sound.
  • Encourage the use of two beaters — one in each hand.
  To remove the bars, use two hands and lift each bar horizontally.

■ *Handchimes, Belleplates, Tonechimes*
  • Play with a short, sharp flick of the wrists. Stop the sound with the other hand.

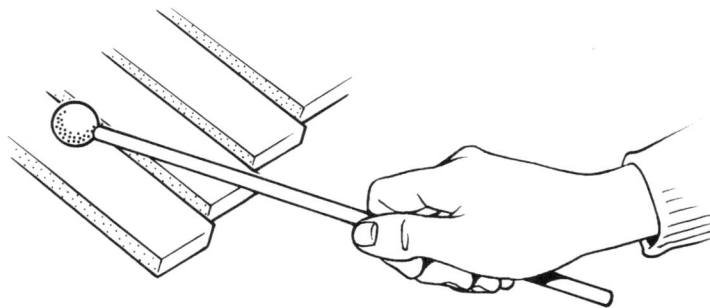

NON-PITCHED INSTRUMENTS

■ *Agogo Bells*
- Hold in one hand and strike with a beater.

■ *Bongo Drums*
- Play with slightly bent fingers — or for a quieter sound, bend fingers more and play with finger tips. Also strike with beaters.

■ *Cabasa*
- Rest in palm of hand; twist handle backwards and forwards with the other hand.
- Alternatively, hold handle with one hand and tap beads with the other.

■ *Castanets*
- Try to use those instruments which have a tight elasticated joint at the base. Pinch them between the fingers and thumb, or rest on a table and tap.
- Castanets on a handle can be held vertically and tapped or shaken.

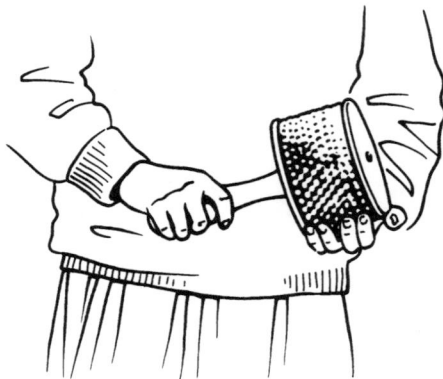

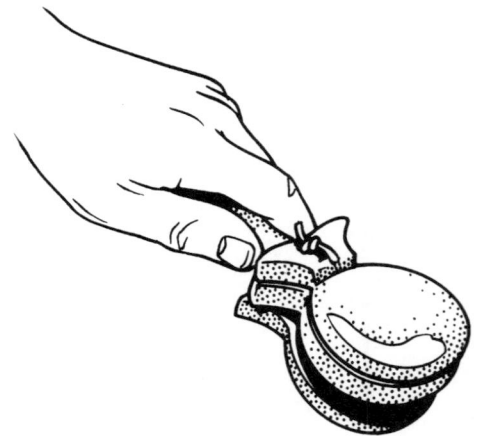

■ *Claves*
- Place one clave across cupped hand forming a 'sound box'. Strike with the other clave. The hollow hand shape will give a greater resonance. This is difficult for small hands; therefore, hold one clave in each hand, and strike against each other.

■ *Cow Bell*
- Hold in one hand and strike with a beater. The cowbell can be mounted on a stand.

■ *Cymbals*
- A suspended cymbal is struck with a beater. To achieve a 'roll', strike alternately with two beaters on opposite sides of the cymbal.
- A pair of cymbals can be clashed together with a swift up and down movement, passing the face of one cymbal across the other. Stop the sound by drawing them into the body.

■ *Flexatone*
  • A short flick of the wrist will allow the beaters to strike either side of the metal plate. Vary the pitch by exerting thumb pressure on the metal plate.

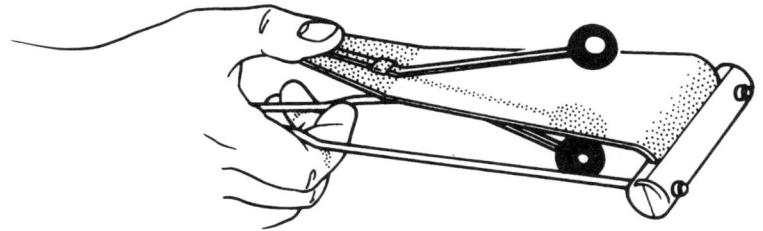

■ *Gato Drum*
  • Strike with rubber beaters, allowing them to bounce.

■ *Indian Bells*
  • Strike one bell with the other. Control the bells by pinching the cord close to the crown.

■ *Jingle Bells*
  • Tap sharply on top of the frame or tap with the jingles held horizontally, or shake for a less precise sound.

■ *Guiro*
  • Draw a scraper along the serrated edge.

■ *Maracas*
  • Either shake sharply using alternate maracas, or hold one maraca facing down and strike the end with the other fist. To achieve a roll, shake the maracas in a circular movement.

■ *Multi Guiro*
  • This can be scraped, shaken, tapped, moved forwards and backwards. It can be tipped to allow the beads/contents to slide around the inside at your chosen speed.

■ Sleigh Bell
- Tap against the hip. Give a sharp shake. For a precise beat, hold with one hand and tap with the other.

■ Tambour
- Play with slightly bent fingers — or for a quieter sound, bend fingers more and play with finger tips. Also play with beaters.

■ Tuneable Tambour
- To ensure an even tension over the skin, slacken all the screws and then tighten them using opposite wing nuts. You can usually 'feel' if each wing nut is the same tension.

■ Tambourine
- Rest horizontally on knee. Tap rhythm sharply on the rim — only the jingles will sound — or hold the tambourine vertically and bounce fingers or thumb on the skin, or shake.

■ Temple Blocks
- Strike sharply with a beater.

■ Triangle
- Grasp the holder close to the triangle and strike the inside of the base or the outside of the top angle. To 'roll', move beater rapidly from side to side inside the top angle.

■ Vibraslap
- Strike the wooden ball sharply with the palm of the hand.

■ *Woodblock*
  • Two tone — Hold and strike either end. Single tone — strike over slit.

■ *Wooden Agogo*
  • Strike or scrape.

USING INSTRUMENTS

Children need to learn to play instruments in a conventional way, using the most effective technique.

This requires practice. The teacher can help by drawing attention to technique when instruments are being used. It does not preclude experimenting with instruments to produce a range of less conventional sounds. Many basic principles still apply, even if, for example, the instrument is being struck in a different place.

These illustrations demonstrate a way of playing the most common classroom instruments to achieve:
• good sound quality — the vibrations are unhindered, allowed to resonate and are projected well;
• good control — the instruments and beaters are positioned and held so that sounds can be produced accurately and confidently;
• good care — good technique is helpful in ensuring that equipment is not accidentally damaged.

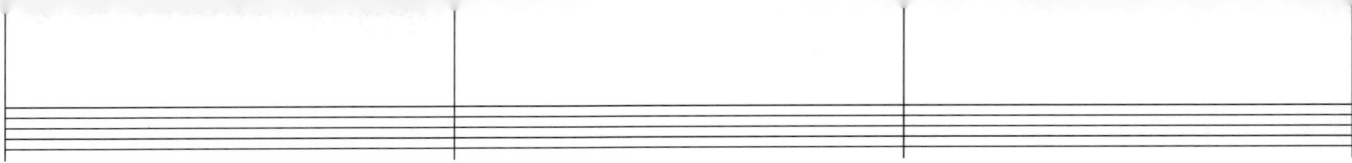

Piano or Organ

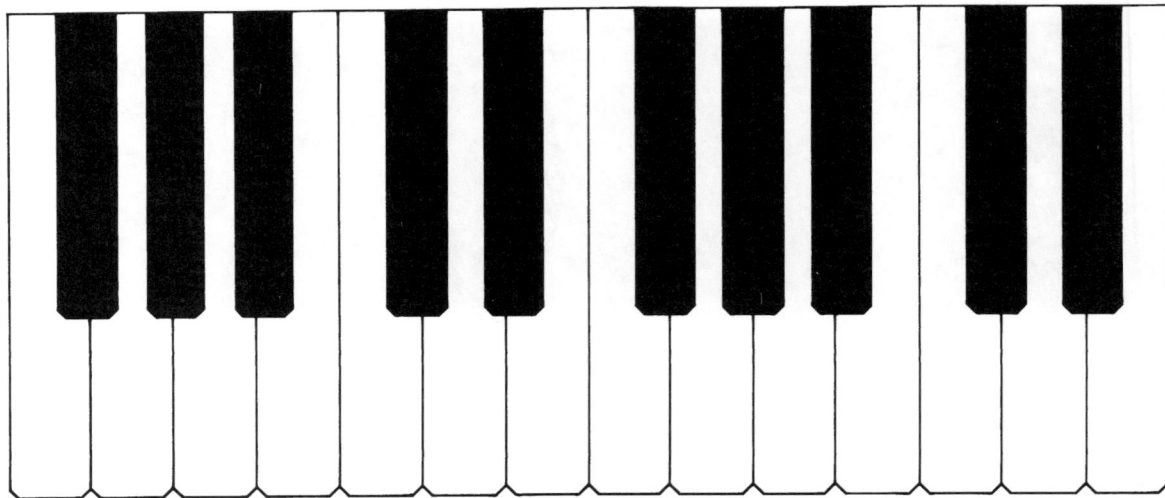

Chime bars or glockenspiel

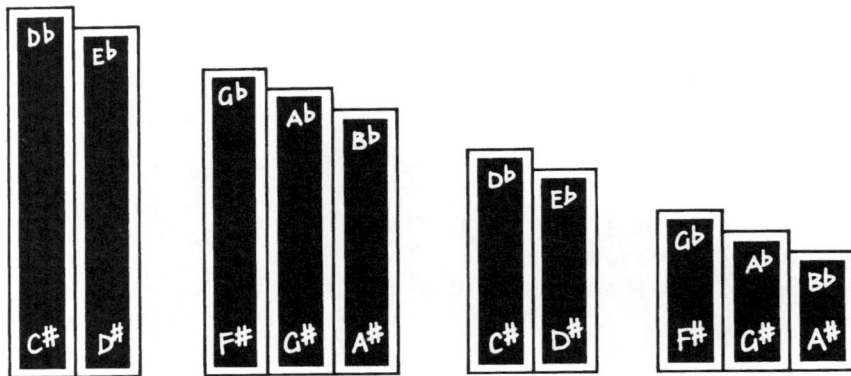

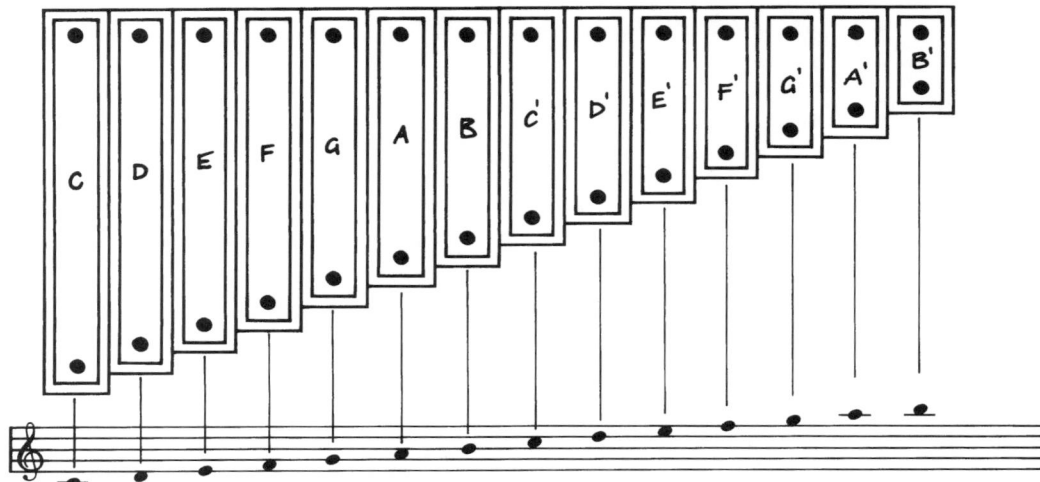

Glossary

For descriptions of musical instruments see page 167.

AB structure
a musical plan that has two different sections.

ABA structure
a musical plan that has three sections. Sections 1 and 3 are the same, section 2 is different.

Accelerando
getting faster.

Accent
a single pitch played or sung with more emphasis than those around it.

Accompaniment
music that supports the sound of the featured performer(s).

Allegro
fast.

Alto
see contralto (can also be a man).

Articulation
clear rhythm (and enunciation of words in singing).

Bar
a group of beats.

Bass
low-pitched man's voice or low-pitched instrument.

Beat
a repeating pulse.

Brass
metal wind instruments (excluding flute and saxophone).

Canon
see In canon.

Chamber music
music for a small group (originally, to be played in a room).

Choral
sung by a chorus.

Chord
group of pitches played simultaneously.

Chorus (1)
see 'refrain'.

Chorus (2)
large group of singers.

Coda
a short 'tail' added at the end of a piece of music.

Compound time
metre where beats are divided into sets of 3, e.g. $\frac{6}{8}$.

Concerto
piece for one or more soloists and orchestra.

Contralto
low female voice.

Contrast
two or more things that are different. In music, slow is a contrast to fast.

Counter-melody
a melody which is played or sung at the same time as another melody.

Crescendo
getting louder.

Diminuendo
getting quieter.

Drone
a continuous or repeated pitch or pitches.

Duet
two singers or players.

Duration
long/short; beat; rhythm.

Dynamics
the loudness and quietness of sound.

Eighth note (♪)
see 'note values'.

Flat ♭
sign indicating that a note should be played a half-step lower.

Form
see 'structure'.

Forte (*f*)
loud.

Fortissimo (*ff*)
very loud.

Found sounds
sounds from sources and objects not necessarily designated musical instruments.

Graphic score
notation using pictures or symbols other than conventional music notation.

Half note (♩)
see note values.

Hand jive
rhythmic sequence of hand movements.

Harmony
two or more different pitches sounding at the same time.

Improvisation
making up music as it is being performed; often used in jazz.

In canon
parts coming in after each other, like a round.

Incidental music
music to accompany a play, which is not central to the action.

Introduction
in a song, music played before the singing starts.

Leap
moving from one pitch to another, skipping the pitches in between, e.g. from D to G (see step).

Libretto
opera words.

Madrigal
secular piece for unaccompanied voices in harmony (mostly 16th century).

Melody
a succession of pitches which has an organised and recognisable shape (tune).

Metre
organisation of strong and weak beats (usually in 2s or 3s).

Mezzo forte (*mf*)
fairly loud.

Mezzo piano (*mp*)
fairly quiet.

Musical
popular stage show involving singing, drama, speech and dance, in costume.

Non-pitched percussion
percussion instruments which do not produce a specific pitch, e.g. tambourine.

Note values
duration of notes:
$1 \times o = 2 \times \downarrow = 4 \times \downarrow = 8 \times \downarrow$

Notes
symbols for sound in music.

Octave
eight pitches, e.g. CDEFGABC.

Opera
dramatic show with singing, usually no speech, in costume.

Operetta
lighter version of opera, often humorous, with speech.

Oratorio
religious work for solo singers, chorus and orchestra.

Orchestra
group of instrumentalists, usually in groups of strings, woodwind, brass and percussion.

Ostinato
a rhythm or melody pattern that is repeated many times, usually as an accompaniment.

Overture
a piece of orchestral music designed to be played at the beginning of a concert, opera or musical.

Pace
see 'tempo'.

Penillion
traditional Welsh form, where the voice sings one melody while the harp plays a different melody simultaneously.

Pentatonic
music based on a 5-pitch scale, e.g. CDEGA.

Percussion
instruments that are played by striking with beaters or by shaking.

Phrase
a musical 'sentence'.

Pianissimo (*pp*)
very quiet.

Piano (*p*)
quiet.

Pitch (1)
a single musical sound.

Pitch (2)
the highness or lowness of sound.

Pitched percussion
percussion instruments which produce a specific pitch or pitches, e.g. chime bar.

Pizzicato
plucked strings.

Pulse
see 'beat'.

Quarter note (♩)
see note values.

Quartet
a group of 4 players or singers.

Rāg
sequence of pitches used in Indian music, e.g. Rāg Bhairav.

Rallentando
getting slower.

Refrain
the part of a song that repeats, with the same melody and words.

Repetition
music that is the same, or almost the same, as music that was heard earlier.

Rest
silence between musical sounds.

Rhythm
the organisation of beat, no beat, long and short sounds, metre, tempo, etc.

Rhythm pattern
a group of long and short sounds, even or uneven sounds.

Ritenuto
getting slower.

Round
a song where different groups of singers sing the same thing, starting at different times.

Scale
an arrangement of pitches from lower to higher (ascending) or higher to lower (descending), according to a specific pattern of steps between them.

Semitone
half-step between two pitches, e.g. F to G.

Solo
music for a single performer, often with an accompaniment.

Soprano
high woman's voice.

Sound quality
see 'timbre'.

Staff/staves
set of 5 lines on which music notes are placed to indicate pitch.

Staccato
pitches played or sung in a short, detached way.

Steady beat
regular pulses. The children clap 'in time'.

Step
moving from one pitch to the next, e.g. from B to C, or F to F# (see leap).

Strings
instruments with strings (usually orchestral: violins, violas, cellos, double basses).

Strong beat
usually the first beat in a bar.

Structure
the overall plan of a piece of music.

Tāl
rhythms pattern used in Indian music, e.g. Rupak Tāl.

Tempo
the speed of the beat in music (fast, slow).

Tenor
high man's voice.

Texture
the way melody and harmony go together, a melody alone, two or more melodies together, or a melody with chords.

Timbre
the special quality of a sound. A flute has a different timbre from a violin.

Time signature
figures at beginning of staff indicating the metre of the music, e.g. = three quarter notes in a bar.

Tone colour
see 'timbre'.

Tremolo
with a tremulous effect.

Triad
chord consisting of three pitches, e.g. CEG.

Treble
child's voice.

Trio
group of three singers or players.

Tuned percussion
see 'pitched percussion'.

Unison
everyone singing or playing the same melody together.

Un-tuned percussion
see 'non-pitched percussion'.

Verse
the part of a song that repeats, with the same melody but different words.

Vocal line
the part of a song which is sung.

Whole note (o)
see note values.

Woodwinds
Wind instruments made of wood (e.g. clarinet, oboe) but also including flute.

Index

Songs and listening extracts

SONGS	UNIT	LESSON	CD	TRACK	PAGE
African chant	5	2	3	4&5	89
Divali Song	2	3	1	13&14	37
Dona Nobis Pacem	4	1	2	11&12	69
Good News	4	4	2	16&17	78
Inch Worm	1	1	1	1&2	12
Magic Bells	4	6	2	21&22	83
Mistletoe and Wine	2	6	1	20&21	45
Music's Mine	5	5	3	8&9	97
Notin' Around	1	3	1	3&4	17
Now Light 1000 Christmas Lights	2	4	1	15	40
Polish the Old Menorah	2	1	1	11&12	33
Silver Moon	1	6	1	7&8	24
Simple Gifts	3	1	2	1	50
Song for Oxum	5	3	3	6	91
Songs of the West	3	6	2	9&10	59
Sumer is Icumen In	4	2	2	13&14	71
Summer Holiday	6	5	3	18	114
Syncopation	5	1	3	2&3	87
Thank You For The Music	6	6	3	19&20	115
This is Our Country	6	7	3	21	120
Turn, Turn, Turn	1	7	1	9&10	27
We're Going to the Country	6	1	3	10&11	104
White Cliffs Of Dover, The	6	2	3	12	105
Workaday Mornin' Blues	3	3	2	6	53
You'll Never Walk Alone	3	5	2	8	58

LISTENING EXTRACTS	UNIT	LESSON	CD	TRACK	PAGE
Anon: The National Anthem	6	7	3	22	120
Are You Listening? Bands	6	4	3	17	111
Are You Listening? Syncopation	5	4	3	7	93
Are You Listening? Gilbert & Sullivan	4	5	2	18	79
Bach: Brandenburg Concerto No 4, Mvt 1 (extract)	1	4	1	5	19
Bach: Chorale Prelude In Dulci Jubilo (organ) (extract)	2	5	1	17	41
Baker/Stone: Ein Schnapps (extract)	6	4	3	15	111
Beethoven: Für Elise (extract)	5	4	3	7	93
Bizet: Farandole from L'Arlésienne	4	3	2	15	75
Coates: Dambusters March (extract)	6	2	3	13	105
Copland: Appalachian Spring (extract)	3	1	2	2	50
Garland/Razaf: In the Mood (extract)	5	1	3	1	87

LISTENING EXTRACTS	UNIT	LESSON	CD	TRACK	PAGE
Gershwin: Summertime from Porgy and Bess	3	2	2	3	51
Gershwin: I've Got Plenty of Nothin' from Porgy and Bess	3	2	2	4	51
Gershwin: Porgy and Bess (extract)	3	2	2	5	51
Gilbert & Sullivan: When the Foeman Bears His Steel, from The Pirates of Penzance (extract)	4	5	2	18	79
Gilbert & Sullivan: Brightly Dawns Our Wedding Day, from The Mikado (extract)	4	5	2	18	79
Gilbert & Sullivan: There is Beauty in the Bellow of the Blast, from The Mikado (extract)	4	5	2	18	79
Gilbert & Sullivan:The Policeman's Song, from The Pirates of Penzance (extract)	4	5	2	19	79
Gilbert & Sullivan: A Paradox, from The Pirates of Penzance (extract)	4	5	2	18	79
Gilbert & Sullivan: A More Humane Mikado, from the Mikado (extract)	4	5	2	18	79
Gray/De-Lange: String of Pearls (extract)	5	4	3	7	93
Handel: The Arrival of the Queen of Sheba (extract)	5	4	3	7	93
Hely-Hutchinson: Carol Symphony, Mvt 1 (extract)	2	5	1	19	41
Mozart: Magic Flute (extract)	4	6	2	20	83
Mozart: A Musical Joke (Rondo)	5	4	3	7	93
Neff/Lewis/Moross: The Big Country (extract)	5	4	3	7	93
Offenbach: The Can-Can (extract)	6	4	3	17	111
Revaux et al: My Way (extract)	6	4	3	16	111
Smyth: The Wreckers Overture (extract)	6	4	3	17	111
Sounds of the Blitz	6	3	3	14	109
Sousa: Sound Off (extract)	6	4	3	17	111
Sousa: The Royal Welch Fusiliers (extract)	6	4	3	17	111
Spear: Coronation Street (extract)	6	4	3	17	111
Trad: Heal the Soul	3	4	2	7	55
Trad, arr Finegan: Little Brown Jug	6	4	3	17	111
Trad: O Come All Ye Faithful	2	5	1	18	41
Trad: In Dulci Jubilo (choral) (extract)	2	5	1	16	41
Vivaldi: The Four Seasons, Winter, Largo (extract)	1	4	1	6	19
Walton: Portsmouth Point (extract)	5	4	3	7	93